Our Family Histories

Hortons, DeHavens, Surratts, Fitzgeralds, & Caves

by

Dean W. Brown

authorHOUSE®

AuthorHouse™
1663 Liberty Drive, Suite 200
Bloomington, IN 47403
www.authorhouse.com
Phone: 1-800-839-8640

First published by AuthorHouse 6/12/2008

ISBN: 978-1-4343-8712-7 (sc)

Library of Congress Control Number: 2008904218

Printed in the United States of America
Bloomington, Indiana

This book is printed on acid-free paper.

The Blue Ridge Mountains, Photo by Gail Josey

A special thanks to Eleanor Brown, Jeanette Martin
for editing assistance.

Photo Cover by Gilmer F. Horton

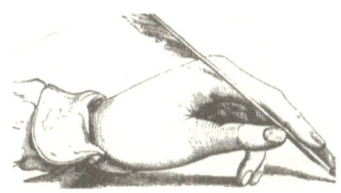

This is a gathering of stories of our families and the Genealogy of 780 years of Hortons, 381 years of DeHavens, 171 years of Fitzgeralds, 291 years of Surratts, and 456 years of Caves. It is in no way complete. It is also in no way one hundred percent perfect. Written records depend upon how well folks kept records and how well those records were recorded. I will continue to make changes as necessary to have a history of our families that we can pass on to our children and be proud of. I am amazed at the accomplishments that our ancestors completed. Many of them did amazing things in a short life span.

If any family members want additions or corrections made in this work, please contact me for changes necessary to make this an accurate account of our history.

I had a great deal of assistance from Sandra Goins Llewellyn, Maxine Grove, Jeanette Brown Martin, Gilmer Horton, Clara Chavier and James Horton.

Footnotes: Information taken from Mormon Records, Ancestor. com, Carroll County Records, Gilmer Horton, Sandra Llewellyn, Dean Brown, Jeanette Brown Martin,. Roots web.com, Maxine Grove, Wikepedia Encyclopedia, Winston Salem Journal, Watauga Democrat, Wytheville News; Family Bibles, Obituary records of Moody Funeral Home, Clara Chavier and James Horton, U. S. Census Records, and US Social Security Death Index.

Dedication

This book is dedicated to those of our families who have served in the Revolutionary And Civil Wars. Their names are listed at the end of this book.

The Horton Family Crest
By Gilmer F. Horton

The Horton coat of arms came into existence centries ago.
The process of creating coats of arms (also called family
crests) began in the eighth and ninth centuries. The new art
of Heraldry made it possible for families and even individual
family members to have their very own coat of arms.

John W. Horton, July 26, 1853 - May 18, 1922

John and Tibitha McMillian Horton,
Born: Sept 7, 1854-January 6, 1935

Michael Marvin Horton, January 27, 1875- July 28, 1934;

Susie Grove and Her Mother
Octavia DeHaven, April 29, 1870

1923 Photo of June Maybery, Minnie Horton, Bob Horton, Katherine Horton, Ruth Horton, Gilmer Horton, Myrtle Horton, Owen Horton, Elmer Horton, Grandma Octavia Horton, Grandma Maybery

1920's Photo of Michael and Octavia Horton, Everett, Arnold, Marvin, May, Pearl, Ray and Susie Horton

Horton Brothers in the 1930's

Horton family farm and mule, Max Meadows, VA

Ray, Pearl, May, Michael and Octavia, Marvin, Fate,
Elmer and Michael Horton

Marvin Chester Horton

Genealogy of Our Horton Family

(Starting with the most recent generation and counting back)

Generation I- Dean Wayne Brown, Born 1938, Married December 27, 1964 to Eleanor Bradley, Born January 30, 1937; Children:

(1) Mark Thomas Brown, Born August 4, 1966; Married: Shasta Bode, Born July 3, 1965, Date of Marriage 1992; Children:

(a) Katherine Elizabeth Brown, Born July 18, 1994;

(b) John-Henry Samuel Brown, Born April 16, 1997

(2) Molly Elizabeth Brown, Born October 8, 1969: Married: Robert Griffin, Date of 1st Marriage July 2, 1994; Children: Dominick Griffin, Born December 24, 2002; 2nd Marriage, March 31, 2007, Robert Robinson, Born August 30, 1973; Children:

(a) Austin Robinson, Born May 20, 1995

Generation II- Katherine Florence Horton, Born June 28, 1920, Wythe County, Virginia, and Died October 5, 2004: The following is an account of her life in her own words, the way she told it. Her family moved to Mount Airy, NC, when she was eleven. She attended Franklin High School. At the age of seventeen, she fell in love and married Thomas Franklin Brown. They were married for 62 years, until his death in 1999. Katherine strived to be a splendid mother and housekeeper. She spent her life looking after the needs of her three children: Dean Brown,

Leon Brown, and Jeanette Brown Chappell. She had 10 grandchildren, and 8 great grandchildren. Jeanette is a retired teacher, Dean is a retired teacher and author of children's books and Leon is an ordained Methodist minister.

When she first married, she worked with her husband in their general store for a brief time, but later elected to stay home with her children. She loved to attend church and was a busy worker at the Mount Carmel Baptist Church where she taught Sunday school, sang in the choir, and was the WMU president. She loved her church work and her friends at Mount Carmel, and continued as long her health permitted. She once said she had a secret desire to play the piano as her daughter did, but was never able to achieve that life goal. After her husband retired they traveled together to Florida and several Southern states. She and her sisters Helen and Jean along with their mother traveled to California, a trip that Katherine spoke of until her death.

Katherine recalled the happiest times of her life were the children and grandchildren coming home for Christmas and getting ready for the event with her special cooking and shopping. She was known for her Christmas cake recipes. Her Applesauce and Fresh Coconut Cakes were the envy of the City of Mount Airy and on occasions she would sell some of them to special families.

Katherine credited her mother's strict teaching and guidance in making her the lady she turned out to be in life. She learned to work hard at a young age and to be respectful and polite to others. She said she had a wonderful life and didn't regret anything. Married: Thomas Franklin Brown, Born 1917, Surry County, North Carolina; Died October 3, 1999; Children:

> (1) Dean Wayne Brown, Born 1938 (See Generation I) Married Eleanor Bradley, December 27, 1964, Children:
>
> > (a) Mark Thomas Brown, Born August 4, 1966; Married February 15, 1992 to Shasta Bode, Born July 3, 1965; Children:
> >
> > > (1) Katherine Elizabeth Brown, Born July 18, 1994;

(2) John-Henry Samuel Brown, Born April 16, 1997

(b) Molly Elizabeth Brown, Born October 8, 1969; Married: 1st Robert Dominick Griffin, Born October 8, 1970 on July 2, 1994, Children:

(1) Dominick Thomas Griffin, Born December 24, 2002; 2nd Marriage: Robert Robinson, Born May 20, 1973. Date of Marriage: March 31, 2007

(2) Roy Leon Brown, Born June 7, 1942; Married Janice Elaine Matthews, Born March 24, 1950; Married June 5, 1965; Children:

(a) Karen Elaine Brown, Born December 5, 1967; Married 1st Keith Helton, 2nd Marriage John Barber; Children:

(1) Brittany Page Helton, Born March 20, 1984;

(2) Brandy Nicolette Helton, Born November 6, 1990

(b) Janice Susan Brown, Born December 5, 1969; Married: 1st Ronald Davis, 2nd Jeffery Bryson, 3rd David Charles Utter Children:

(1) Julia Davis,

(2) Megan Davis

(3) Living Son

(c) Phillip Roy Brown

(d) David Matthew Brown, Born December 5, 1973; Married Jackie Lloyd, Born January 1, 1972; Children:

(1) Carisia Danielle Brown, Born September 24, 2000;

(2) Colby Matthew Brown, Born November 23, 2003

(e) Michael Leon Brown, Born September 1, 1975; Married Lorraine Brown; Children:

(1) Christian Michael Brown, Born May 13, 2000;

        (2) Caitlin Lorraine Brown, Born January 7, 2004

    (f) Timothy Gabriel Brown, Born March 25, 1982

(3) Jeanette Brown Chappell Martin, Born June 16, 1945; Married 1st Otis Chappell, Born March 20, 1943; Died February 13, 2003; Children:

    (a) Stephanie Kathleen Chappell, Born November 21 1970;Married David Warren McDuffie, Born February 15, 1968; Married: September 13, 1997; Children:

        (1) Kathleen Claire (Katie) McDuffie, Born February 27, 2002

        (2) Reece Tillman McDuffie, Born August 12, 2003

    (b) Julie Anna Chappell, Born August 17, 1973; Married James Stanley Marion, Born February 13, 1968; Marriage June 5, 1998; Children:

        (1) Anna Elizabeth Marion, Born September 30, 1999;

        (2) Meredith Craig Marion, Born January 9, 2002;

        (3) James Stanley Marion, Jr., Born December 7, 2004; 2nd Marriage to Clinton Martin May 5, 2007

The Birthday Party

Marvin and Annie with Grandchildren Debbie,
Sandra, Jeanette, Leon and Dean 1950

Generation III- Marvin Chester Horton, Born June 6, 1897; Died January 24, 1964. Forsyth County, NC. Grandpa Horton was a tall heavy man who would have probably weighed over 300 pounds. Being tall, he carried his weight well. He had an accident when he was a young boy working with logs in the mountains and damaged his hip and legs. He had managed to recover without much medical attention but walked with a heavy limp and always used crutches. Sometimes he walked with one crutch and sometimes he used two crutches, according to how much pain he was feeling on that particular day. He suffered his entire life with severe pain from the logging accident. He spoke loudly with a deep voice and could be heard over anyone else that was talking. The corners of his mouth turned up in such a way that one would translate into a half-smile even when he was serious. He chewed Brown's Mule Tobacco and usually had some in his mouth with a few drops showing in the corners of his mouth. I always thought he was an intelligent man. He was open to new ideas and would become interested in anything new or ideas which I had to talk about. Once he ordered a donkey from Sears and Roebuck, bought a camera and tried making pictures of children at events. He had no way to haul the donkey except in the back seat of his car, which he had won at a drawing at the Surry County Fair. It was a funny sight to see him driving down the road with the donkey looking out the back seat window. He had a love for dogs, horses, friends and telling tall tales. Married: Annie Myrtle Surratt, Born January 29, 1897; Died February 25, 1982.

Grandmother Horton was a kind, soft spoken lady with a raspy voice. She was a devout Christian lady and attended Mount Carmel Baptist Church. She sat in the "a-men" corner, which was a section for older folks at the front of the church. Sometimes she would let the grandchildren sit with her. She enjoyed singing the old time hymns and could be heard singing in her kitchen most of the time when we grandchildren visited. She made her own soap, scrubbed her clothes on a washboard and a hand wringer washing machine. She was especially fond of her chickens. Each one had a name and a special place in her heart. She sold some of their eggs for extra money. She would kill and fry the chickens for company but never ate one herself. She raised her own hogs for meat. On hog killing day, usually about the first of November she would work up the meat. There were hams and shoulders that she would salt cure, hand grind her own sausage, render the fat from the "leftovers" to make "chitlens" and lard. She was a wonderful cook.

Her vegetable garden was the envy of the ladies of the neighborhood as she would preserve hundreds of jars or vegetables and fruit. She also dried apples for her wonderful fried apple pies. She kept a cow in a neighbor's pasture close by. She made her own butter, and sold milk to some of the neighbors. There was no central heat in her house so her kitchen was heated with her cook stove. She used little wood sticks which she chopped by herself. Her sitting room had a warm morning heater that used wood and coal. There was a larger coal stove in the living room, which she would heat up only for special company or the quilting ladies. During the winter they would meet one day each week for an afternoon of quilting. Most of the ladies bought feed bags for their animals that had designs on them. The bags were made into dresses, shirts, etc., and the left over pieces would be used to piece together a quilt. The quilts were mostly heavy and were used on beds for winter. There was no heat in the bedrooms. Grandma worked very hard keeping her house and children in clothing. She taught them morals and Christian beliefs which have been passed down to her grandchildren.

She was a great story teller, especially scary stories. That was one way to keep the grandchildren quiet when we stayed with her. She was never known to smile very much; actually it was rare to hear her laugh. She never spoke very much of her childhood. Even when I questioned her, she gave a very brief story. She says that her mother went "crazy" and the brothers and sisters had to be placed in different homes. A check of some of the early census records actually record that grandma was four years old and living in a grandparent's home near Lead Mines, Virginia. She married very young in order to escape the living conditions. She never complained about any situation she found herself in during her life. As she aged and her joints became stiff, she would sit at home and listen to the Radio and TV. She liked to read and do some needle work. When her grapes ripened, we told her that we would pick them this time, but she climbed on a chair and picked them anyway. The chair fell and she broke her hip severely and never walked very much after that. She passed away in the Surry Community Nursing Home. Children:

Jean Horton about 1945

Gilmer F. Horton,
4th grade

(1) Gilmer Fred Horton, Ret. T-Sergeant, US Air Force, Born 1917; Died 1982, Gilmer graduated from Franklin High School in Surry County and entered Mount Airy High School the next year. The principal at Mount Airy wanted to know why he wanted two diplomas.

After Gilmer explained that he needed Latin, Physics, Chemistry, Algebra, mechanical drawing and some other important courses that he had not received at his previous High School, he was permitted to enter and he did receive a diploma from Mount Airy High School in 1938. After his graduation from Mount Airy High, Gilmer pursued a career with the US Department of Justice. There is a copy of a letter from J. Edgar Hoover related to this inquiry. In 1953 he was discharged from the US Air Force.

Gilmer's most significant assignment during that service was listed as Hq. 98th Bomb Wing (SAC). He served in France, Tunisian and Sicilian campaigns. He was Mount Airy's first volunteer. His medals and commendations included: Good Conduct Medal w/2 Loops, National Defense Service Medal, Commendation Ribbon w/Metal Pendant, Korean Service Medal, and United Nations Service Medal. He received a Military Training Certificate from Fort Bragg in Field Artillery. After his discharge in 1945, he reentered the US Army and was assigned to the Intelligence division in the United Kingdom where he earned the World War II Victory Medal. His next service was with the United States Air Force, earning the Army of Occupational Medal, American Defense Medal, Good Conduct Medal, EAME Campaign Medal, and the American Thea Medal. Not much is known about the intelligence work; however it is known that it carried him all over the world.

One document reads: "Assisted in the collection evaluation interpretation and distribution of information of enemy and counter-intelligence activities and the safe guarding of military information." There is a personal note from Harry S. Truman, commending him on his performance. Another citation from the 9th Infantry Division states the following: "On the night of the 14th of August, 1943, in the City of Cesaro, Sicily, awakened by explosions and resultant fire from an enemy bombing attack, and fire of the ammunition dump at the AMGOT Headquarters and the building housing the public records of the country. Gilmer immediately seized the initiative and by valorous and aggressive efforts extinguished the flames, thereby eliminating a possible disaster. His performance, at great risk to his own safety, merits high commendations".

He was an inventor and is credited with an invention of a fuel valve that regulated the flow of fuel in jet engines. This invention was adapted by Canada, United Kingdom, and France, but was never used in the USA. Gilmer enjoyed doing research, and is credited with designing several medals for the US Air Force.

Gilmer loved his family and especially nephews and nieces. He always drew his own Christmas Cards that he sent to us. He never married; however, I do know of several loves he had before and after he retired in his later years. He loved guns, and always carried one for protection along with two rottweiler dogs, even when he took his daily strolls in the woods. After his death, even though the dogs knew me very well and were friendly toward me, they would not let me in the house, and I had to pay to have them "done away with" before I could enter the house. He loved to travel back to his home place in Max Meadows, and he and I made that trip many times. He always kept a daily journal, and that collection can be seen at the Mount Airy Museum of Regional History, in Mount Airy, NC. Gilmer died of cancer and was buried in Oakdale Cemetery, Mount Airy, NC.

Ruth Horton Made about 1935

(2) Ruth Horton Goins, Born 1918; Died May 4, 1988; Married Buddy Isaac Goins, Born August 7, 1920; Died March 4, 2005; Children:

    (a) Sandra Ann Goins, Born June 23, 1950; Married Larry Thomas Llewellyn in April 4, 1979

Katherine Horton Photo made about 1936

(3) Katherine Horton, Born June 28, 1920; Died October 5, 2004; Married: Thomas Franklin Brown; Born August 9, 1917; Died October 3, 1999; Children:

    (a) Dean Wayne Brown, Born November 26, 1938,

(b) Roy Leon Brown, Born June 7, 1942,

(c) Ann Jeanette Brown, Born June 16, 1945

(Detailed information see Generation I and II)

Helen and Arnold Draughn

(4) Helen Horton, Born July 15, 1922, Died February 28, 2008; Married August 9, 1944 to Arnold V. Draughn, Born January 29, 1920, North Carolina; Died May 14, 1997

Mazie Horton Photo About 1945

(5) Mazie Goldie Horton, Born March, 2, 1924 and Died October 25, 2006; Married: Tommy Dara, Born July 16, 1910; Died Aug 23, 1985, Vero Beach, Florida, Mazie worked for the Bell Telephone company after World War II in Baltimore, Md. She later moved to Miami Beach, Florida, where she met Tommy Dara who was owner of Dara Construction. They built a lovely home in Carol Gables, Florida where they raised their family. Children:

(a) Deborah Ann Dara, Born April 1, 1951; Married Hank Pohl August 2, 1975; Children:

(1) Heather Ann Pohl, Born September 17, 1980; Children; Makenzie Alma Dara

(b) Steven Dara, Born March 10, 1955

Dan Horton About 1940

(6) Daniel C. Horton, Born October 10, 1926, Wythe County, Virginia; Died January 5, 1992, Miami, Florida. Married Frances Horton; Died July 2006; Children:

(a) Daniel Chester Horton, Born January 23, 1950, Married Elizabeth Frances Raul; Children:

    (1) Robin Angela Horton, Born August 20, 1981;

(b) Kenneth Michael Horton, Born November 7, 1955,

(c) Richard Francis Horton, Born April 6, 1961

Jean Horton
Photo made 1941

(7) Jean Horton, Born June 8, 1932; Married: (Gus) Ural Sigmon Gabriel; Born 1928; Died August 8, 1990; Children:

(a) Scott Alan Gabriel, Born January 15, 1961, Children:

    (1) Zachary Aaron Gabriel, Born Nov. 19, 1990

    (2) Jacob Allen Gabriel, Born February 19, 1994;

(b) Bryan Phillip Gabriel, Born July 1, 1963

Generation IV- Michael Marvin Horton, Born January 27, 1875; Died July 28, 1934; Wife: Octavia DeHaven, Born April 29, 1870, Carroll County, Virginia; Died June 19, 1959, Carroll County, Virginia. Michael died of a heart attack, after visiting his children in Mount Airy. He awoke Saturday Morning not feeling well and asked Rupert to drive him back to Max Meadows. On the trip back he became very ill. In the middle of the New River Bridge, Elizabeth felt of his forehead and said, "Everett your daddy is dead!" They stopped at a station after they crossed the New River Bridge at Jackson's Ferry where a neighbor came out of the house next door and took the children in the house. An ambulance was called and he was taken to the Wytheville Hospital, but he was dead on arrival. He is buried at Mountain Plains Cemetery, Carroll County, Virginia, Children:

(1) Rupert Everett Horton, Born March 23, 1895, Died 1967; Wife: Elizabeth Midkiff Horton, Born September, 13, 1898, Died July 21, 1996; Children:

    (a) Virginia Pauline Horton, Born August 5, 1922, Surry County; Died 1924

    (b) Hazel Marie Horton, Born: May 12, 1920, Died: September 18, 2004; Married: Robert Glenn Lawrence, Born May 20, 1920; Died August 5, 1984 Southern Pines, NC; Children:

        (1) Pearl Elizabeth Lawrence, Married: Michael Orr,

        (2) Martin "Mart" Edward Lawrence, Married: Sue Ellen Truelove,

        (3) Shelia Joan Lawrence, Married: Gary "Steve" McNeill,

        (4) Robert Dale Lawrence, Married: Teresa Jackson 1st and Ann Bass 2nd

    (c) Sadie Bell Horton, Born October 24, 1939; Married Donald Evans Spargo, Sr.; Children: Donald Evans Spargo, Jr.

    (d) Rupert Clarence Horton, Born August 23, 1926; Married Edith Payne; Children:

        (1) Michael Ray Horton, one child,

        (2) Judy Ann Horton (Brown), one child,

        (3) Debra Sue Horton (Inman), one child,

        (4) Ronald Horton, one child,

(5) Brenda Gail Horton (Wall), one child; Larry Dean Horton

(e) Clara Horton, Born April 2, 1930, Married (Joe) Joseph Chavier, Born September 27, 1920, Mass.; Died February 9, 2007.

(f) James Clifford Horton, Born 1937; Married Carol Johnson, Born October 24, 1939; Children:

(1) Joseph Anthon Horton (Joey),

(2) William Jefferson Horton (Jeff),

(3) James Clifford Horton, Jr. (Jamey)

Ethel Mabry, Susie Horton, Edith Mabry, May Horton,
Pearl Horton and others not identified

(2) Marvin Chester Horton, Born 1897; Died 1964; Married: Annie Myrtle Surratt, Born January 29, 1897, Died February 25, 1982; Children:

(a) Gilmer Horton (see generation III)

(b) Ruth Horton (see generation III)

(c) Katherine Horton (see generation III)

(d) Helen Horton (see generation III)

(e) Mazie Horton (see generation III)

(f) Daniel Horton (see generation III)

(g) Jean Horton (see generation III)

(3) Pearl Telipha Horton, Born April 26, 1914; Died February 1984; Married: Charles Brown; Children:

(a) June Brown

(4) Elmer Elis Horton, Born December 9, 1915; Died August 3, 1984; Married: (?) Dumpford; Elmer Served in WW II, he was a private and served as a Warrant Officer. Children:

(a) Elmer E. Horton, Jr. of Richmond, Virginia

(5) Wilford Arnold Horton, Born June 6, 1905; Died March 5, 1973; Married: Bessie V. Phebes, Born 1903, Died 1993. Wilford served in WWI and WWII. Wilford and Bessie were in the grocery business for over 30 years. They were owners and operators of the Horton's Trading Post on Newbern Road in Pulaski County. They were known to specialize in groceries, meats and produce. They loved living in Pulaski and spent their life there with the people they have dealt with in business over the years. They enjoyed gardening and just being at home. Children:

(a) Orbra C. Horton, Born 1927, Pulaski, Virginia

(b) Aubrey Clinton Horton; Born December 12, 1916, Died August 1985; Married Betty Queensbury; Children:

(1) Aubrey Horton

(2) Kathy Horton

(c) Minnie Octavia Horton, Married Earnest Montgomery; No Children

(d) Willie Owen Horton, Born 1927, Pulaski, VA; Married: Goldie May Hall; Children:

    (1) Willie Owen, Jr. Born October 18, 1941; Married: Betty Elaine Snyder; Children: Robert Owen Horton, Born August 24, 1964; Dent Prescott Horton Died 1980; Amanda Sue Horton

(e) Thelma Horton Married: William Watson

(f) Robert Franklin (Bob) Horton; Married Kathleen Roseberry; Robert was killed in WWII, April 18, 1944; Children:

    (1) Bobbie Jean Horton

    (2) Brenda Jo Horton

(g) Myrtle Horton, Married Mack Dulton; Children; Patty Sue

(h) Richard Pierce Horton, Married Bonnie Davis; Children:

    (1) Virginia Faye Horton, Married Melton Akers; Children: Bonnie Horton (now deceased); Richaard Horton, Married Nancy Davis

    (2) Robert Long Horton, Married Wanda Sue Reeves; Children: Rickey Horton, Robbie Horton, Rhonda Sue Horton

    (3) Richard Pierce Horton, Jr; Married Brenda Hubbard; Children: Garylee Horton, Steven Horton

(i) James Edwaard Horton (deceased)

(j) Linda Kay Horton, Married Roy Blevens; Children: James Blevens, Brian Blevins, Lea Blevins Sonny Blevins

(k) Janet Elizabeth Horton

(l) Debbie Ann Horton Married Decon Derun

(m) Jerry Duanne Horton Married Glena Horton

(n) Steven Horton (deceased)

(o) David Lee Horton Married Shelly (no information available)

(6) Susan Leanona Horton, Born June 6, 1903; Died 1993. Aunt Susie, as we all called her was a delight to be around. She was always a bundle of energy and a very intelligent lady. She took college classes at night, and during summer to get her BS in Education at Radford University. She taught school in Max Meadows for many years and was loved by all. She was active in her church and community affairs. She always had a funny story to tell everyone. One of her most famous was the story of a chicken in a brown bag that she carried on a train from Radford back to Max Meadows. Married in 1926 to Robert W. Grove, Born 1896, Died 1974. Children:

(a) Edwin William Grove, Born June 15, 1927, Died November 20, 2000; Married Maxine Irwin, Born July 30, 1926. Marriage June 3, 1946. Children:

(1) Edwin William Grove, Jr. Born July 5, 1947

(2) Ronald Irwin Grove, Born March 22, 1949

(b) Robert Horton Grove, Born March 31, 1934; Married Opal Virginia Taylor, November 10, 1954; Children:

(1) Karen Lee Grove, Born September 11, 1955; Married Jonathan David Austin; Children

(a) Sarah Taylor Austin

(b) Rachel Austin

(c) Rebecca Emily Austin

(2) Michael Tayler Grove, Born June 6, 1958

(3) John Cayton (stepson)

Grove family gathering. Included is Robert Grove and
his two sons Edwin Grove and Robert Horton Grove

(7) Early Raymond Horton (Ray), Born 1911, Led Mines VA;
Married: Ollie Jackson; Children:

   (a) Don Horton

   (b) Joyce Horton

   (c) Julian Horton

(8) George Lafayette Horton (Fate); Married: Beulah Coperhaver;
Children:

   (a) William Horton

   (b) Dewey Horton

   (c) Christine Horton

(9) Daisy Lee Horton, Born 1912; Died: April 20, 1914.

(10) May Horton, Married Mr. Mabry Children:

      (a) Thomas Mabry, Jr.; Married Ruby Mabry

Generation V- John W. Horton, Born: July 26, 1853, Carroll County,
Virginia; Died: May 18, 1922; Married: Tibitha McMillian, Born: Sept
7, 1854; Died: January 6, 1935, Carroll County, Virginia. Tabitha was

described as a kind, loving mother and friend to all around her. She was known for her stories of the mountains. They lived in a log cabin just over the top of Fancy Gap Mountain. She went to the outhouse and fell when she was returning and severely broke her hip. She was never able to get around again by herself and died soon afterwards. Children:

(1) Michael M. Horton, Born: June 27, 1875; Died: July 28, 1934; Married: Octavia DeHaven; Children:

    (a) R.E. Horton (Everett),

    (b) M. C. Horton,

    (c) Pearl Horton,

    (c) Elmer E. Horton,

    (d) W. Arnold Horton,

    (e) Susana Horton,

    (f) Ray Horton,

    (g) G.L. (Fate) Horton,

    (h) May Horton,

    (i) Daisy Horton.

(2) Greenville Mc Horton, Born 1876

(3) Jacob W. Horton, Born November 1870; Died: January 27, 1885

(4) Charles Alfred Horton (REV), Born Dec. 8, 1883; Married: Dina Hall September 4, 1906; Children:

    (a) Obediah Horton,

    (b) Paul Horton,

    (c) Woodson Horton,

    (d) Mrs. Emmett Haymore,

(e) Mrs. Arnold Weddle,

(f) Mrs. Avery Boone.

Generation VI- Jacob Horton, Born 1820, Carroll County, Virginia; Died 1890, Carroll County, Virginia, Buried Mountain Plains, Virginia; Married: Margaret Phibbs, Died: 1876. Children:

(1) Charles W. Horton, Born 1848, Died 1924, Buried at Mountain Plains, Virginia.

(2) Martha Lavinia Horton, Born: 1849, Died: 1907, Children:

    (a) Nancy Horton, Died: 1851,

    (b) Johanna Horton,

    (c) Ruben Horton,

    (d) Abraham Horton.

(3) John W. Horton, Born 1853, Died 1880

(4) Charles Horton

(5) Jefferson T. Horton, Born 1855

(6) Eli. Horton, Born 1857, Died 1934

(7) Lucinda Horton, Born 1860

(8) Thomas Horton, Born 1867

Generation VII- Joseph Horton, Born 1780, Surry County, NC; Died December 22, 1876, Carroll County, Virginia, Burial: Thompson Cemetery on Snake Creek; Served in the Confederate Virginia Militia; Married Mary Webb, Born 1785, Died 1876; Children:

(1) Abraham Horton

(2) John Horton, 61st Virginia Infantry, Private, Confederate Army

(3) Rachel Horton, Born January 3, 1807

(4) Benjamin Horton, Born 1804, Died 1887, Carroll County, VA.; Married: Mary Largen; Confederate Virginia Militia of Carroll County, Virginia; Children:

(a) Anna Horton, 1825;

(b) Lucy Horton, 1832;

(c) Henry Horton, 1833;

(d) Vincent Horton, 1835;

(e) Isabel Horton, 1838;

(f) Rachel Horton, 1838;

(g) Jacob Horton, 1841.

(5) James Horton, Born 1802, Grayson County, Virginia

(6) Susanna Horton, Born June 1, 1809

(7) Henry Horton, Born 1811, Grayson County, Virginia; Served: Company K, 16th Virginia Cavalry, Sergeant, Confederate Army, Ferguson's Battn., Va.

(8) Lucy Horton, Born Jan. 1, 1814

(9) Isaac Horton, Born Jan 1, 1816

(10) Jacob Horton, Born Jan 1, 1812; Served: 1st Battalion, Va. Infantry, Private in the Confederate Army

(11) Mary Horton, Born: 1821

(12) Joseph Horton, Born: Jan. 1, 1821; Served: Carroll County, Virginia Militia, Confederate Army.

(13) Andrew Horton, Born: January 2, 1828

(13) William Riley Horton, Born: September 24, 1831

(14) Rubin Horton, Born: 1821

(15) Johanna Horton, Born: 1828

Generation VIII- John Brissell Horton, Born about 1748, Bucks, Pennsylvania; Died 1827, St. Francis, Missouri. John was dismissed from the Westfield Quaker Meeting for marrying Anna who was not a Quaker. Married Anna Green, Born 1756, Guilford, North Carolina; Children:

(1) Joseph Horton, born 1782, Surrey County, NC; Died 1875, Carroll County, Virginia; He was dismissed from the Westfield Quaker Meeting in November 1801 for marrying out of unity. He married Mary Webb, who was born in Grayson County, Virginia. Mary Died 8786, Carroll County, Virginia

(2) Rachel Horton, Born 1782, Died 1885, Surry Co, NC, Married: Giles Webb, Born 1790, Died 1860, West Virginia

(3) John Bissell Horton, Born 1789, Pendleton, Anderson, South Carolina, Died 1870, Washington, Missouri

(4) Leah Horton, Born 1776, Surry County, North Carolina

(5) Hezikah Horton, Born 1808, Pendleton, Anderson, South Carolina; Died 1890, Missouri

(6) Unknown Horton

Generation IX- Abram Horton (Abraham Horton), Born 1722, Mass.; Died June 1, 1816, Surry County, NC; He was a Quaker and died at age 94. Served: American Rev. War as a Private in the Maryland Troops Married: Martha Brissell Williams, Born 1725, Surry County, NC; Died 1808, Westfield, Surry County, NC. Children:

(1) William B. Horton, Born 1746; Served: Carpal in American Rev. Wa.

(2) Daniel B. Horton, Born 1748, Bucks, Pa.

(3) James Horton, Born March 27, 1755, Bucks, PA; Served: American Rev. War as Private in Continental Troops

(4) Priscella Horton

(5) Abraham Brissell Horton, Born May 14, 1759, Bucks PA; Served: Captain in American Rev. War, Continental Troops

(6) Issac Brissell Horton

(7) Mary Elizabeth Horton, Born 1770

Wife #2, Martha Williams, Born 1723

(8) William B. Horton, Born 1763, Bucks Pa; Fought in Rev. War, lived in New York, later moved to Tennessee as a pioneer

(9) Mary Elizabeth Horton, Born 1770

Generation X- John Horton, Born 1662, Springfield, Hampton, Ma.; Died 1763; Married; Wife # 1 Unknown, Birth 1700; Wife #2 Mary Orton, Born 1692, Woodbury, Litchfield, CT; Died 1784; Children:

(1) Abram Horton, Born 1722, Woodbury, CT; Death 1816, Surry, North Carolina; Served: Sergeant American Revolutionary War, Continental Troops; Married: Martha Brissell Williams, Born 1725, Surry, NC; Died 1808, Westfield, Surry, NC; Children:

(a) Abraham Horton,

(b) John Horton,

(c) Rachel Horton,

(d) Benjamin Horton,

(e) James Horton,

(f) Susanna Horton,

(g) Henry Horton, Served: Lieutenant American Revolutionary War, Virginia Troops;

(h) Lucy Horton,

  (i) Isaac Horton,

  (j) Jacob Horton,

  (k) Mary Horton,

  (l) Andrew Horton,

  (m) William Riley Horton.

(2) Joseph Horton, Served: Captain American Revolutionary War, New York Troops

(3) Sara Orton Horton, Born 1723, Woodbury CT

(4) John Orton Horton, Born October 5, 1729, Woodbury, CT

(5) Elizabeth Orton Horton, Born December 8, 1741, Woodbury, CT

(6) Mary Orton Horton, Born February 23, 1741, Woodbury, Litchfield, CT

Generation XI- John Horton, Born June 29, 1672, Winsor, CT, USA; Married: Sarah Hall; Springfield, MA, 1667, Children:

(1) John Horton, Born: November 27, 1700, New Haven, CT, USA

(2) Mary Horton, Born: 1703

(3) Sarah Horton, Birth: 1712, Windsor, CT, USA

(4) Abigail Horton, Born 1714

(5) Samuel Horton, Born 1716, Windsor, CT, USA; Served: Corporal American Rev. War, Continental Troops.

(6) John Horton, Born March 21, 1609, Bristol, MA, USA

Generation XII- Jeremiah Horton, Born August 18, 1636, Died August 28, 1682, Windsor, CT; Married: Wife #1, Mary Wright, Born 1636, MA, CT, Died 1720, Wife #2, Mary Gibbard, Born January 20, 1644,

New Haven, CT, Died October 15, 1708, Springfield Hampden, MA, Mary was the daughter of William Gibbard and Ann Tapp. She was christened on January 20, 1644; New Haven CT. Records reveal the following "Last Will and Testament of her husband": "In the name of God Amen, February 19, 1686, according to the computation of ye Church of England, I Benjamin Horton, in ye County of Suffolk in ye Province of N. Yorke on Long Island, being in perfect memory, do make and ordain this my last will and testament. Item: I give to Caleb, Joshua, Jonathan, and Mersey Youngs, 80 bushels of wheate and Indian, 20 swine, 20 sheep, to be divided to them four alike. I give my house and land, and meadow except my Meadow of Common over the river to the Sacrament table yearly for evermore. I give ten oxen for a bell for the meeting-house to call ye people to worship the Lord God. I give the rest to the poor." Children:

(1) Nathaniel Horton, Born June 29, 1662, Springfield, Hampton, MA, Died September 1667, Springfield, MA

(2) Jeremiah Horton, Born 1665, Hampton, MA

(3) Samuel Johnson Horton, Born Sept 1667, Springfield, MA

(4) Thomas Horton, Born November 30, 1668, Springfield, MA

(5) Timothy Horton, Born 1670, Springfield, MA

(6) John Horton, Born September 12, 1672, Springfield, MA

(7) Mary Horton, Born July 20, 1674; Known as widow Mary Horton possessed much property and Guardian of some of the Horton Children, which was unusual at that time.

(8) Sarah Horton, Born 1677, Springfield, Hampden, MA

(9) Jeremiah Horton, Born 1678

(10) Benjamin Horton, Born October 20, 182, Springfield, MA

Generation XIII- Thomas Horton, Born 1602, Mosley, England, Died 1649 Ireland; He was an English soldier in the parliamentary army during the English Civil War. He was taken under the wing of the powerful Sir Arthur Haselirg, and had become a colonel by 1643. His troops played a decisive part in several important engagements, most notably the Battle of Naseby in 1645 and Battle of St Fagan's in 1648. As a reward for the valiant service he rendered at the cause, Horton was granted the confiscated lands of a deposed royalist. Horton was a commissioner of the high court of justice in 1649 and thus was among those who signed the warrant for the execution of King Charles I of England. Later that year, he died of natural causes while serving with Cromwell in Ireland. His heirs were deprived of their estate at the restoration. Wife Mary Eddy, Born March 10, 1508, Nayland, Suffolk, England; Died September 10, 1683; Children:

(1) Jeremiah Horton, Born 1636, Died 1682; Captain Jeremy Horton, Master and Owner of the ship "The Swallow"

(2) Thomas Horton, Born 1638, USA, Springfield, MA; Died 1693; Thomas was one of the founders of Springfield, Mass. He and his wife came to America on the ship "Mary and John". They settled in Windsor, Connecticut, two or three years, where their son was born. They were educated people. Their signatures are still to be seen in the "Pyncheon Papers" that have to do with land purchase from the Indians.

Thomas was one of the founders of Springfield, Mass.; was witness and signer of the Indian Deed; was town officer and proprietor. His lands are minutely described in History of Springfield, MA. Records show that Thomas Horton was party to a trivial suit at law with Mirick Another.

(3) Mary Horton, Born 1629, England

(4) John Horton, Born 1640

Generation XIV- Joseph De Horton, Born 1572, First House, Burksland, Halifax, England; Died 1640, Springfield, Hampton County, MA; Married, Mary Schuyler in Mowsley, Leicestershire, England, about 1578; Children:

(1) Barnabas Horton, Born July 13, 1600, Mowsley, Leicestershire, England; Died 1680. "The heritage of Barnabas has been carried on through generations from Southold to Salem. Barnabas immigrated about 1635, destination: Hampton, MA

Barnabas immigrated to America in the ship "The Swallow." He landed in at Hampton, Mass., where he owned a plot of ground. He came to New Haven, 1640, with his wife, Mary and two children and settled permanently on the east end of long Island, now Southold, Suffolk County, NY. in October, 1640. He was known as the man of unquestionable character and great faith, which is shown on his table stone and in his will. He became a freeman in Hartford before arriving in Southold where he served as a constable and then as a Deputy to the General Court in 1663 and 1664.

He is known as a founding father of the town and of the church. He was active in the affairs of the church and the colony. It is said that he agreed to maintain the lane to the dock, which allowed him to have lots on either side of Horton's Lane. In 1640 he received a land grant which included the land on which the Horton's Point Lighthouse now sits.

Barnabas is buried in Southold, Suffolk County, NY in the old Burying Ground of the First Presbyterian Church. He married Anne Smith. She was born about 1602 and died in 1630. He then married Mary Langton about 1631 in England and she died in1698.

Barnabas was one of the 13 founding members of Southold, Long Island. In 1640 a small band of Puritans who just a few years before had crossed the Atlantic from many parts of England in search of religious freedom and a better life, became dissatisfied with conditions in New England and secured for themselves a parcel of land across the waters of the Sound on which to organize their church. Led by their pastor the Rev. John Youngs, this group of 13 Englishmen with their families gathered up their cattle and few possessions and set out by sloop or oared barrage from New Haven. They crossed Long Island Sound, sailed up the Peconic Bay and came ashore at Founder's Landing and there in what is today the

Village of Southold, established the first permanent settlement in New York State. (From the history of Greenport)

Several times he served as a member of the General Court of New Haven and Hartford, under whose jurisdiction Southold came at that time."

Children:

(a) Caleb Horton, Born December 22, 1687, Southold, Suffolk County, NY; Died: August 6, 1772, Roxbury (Chester), NJ; Married Phebe Terry, Born June 5, 1690; Died: December 24, 1776. Both are buried in the Chester Congregational Church Yard in Morris County, NJ.

(b) Colonel Nathan Horton, Born 1720, Southold, Suffolk County, NY; Died: August, 1807, Roxbury (Chester), NJ Married Mehetable Case, 1749, South Suffolk, NY. Captain Nathan Horton served in the Revolutionary War after moving to Roxbury, NJ from Southold, Suffolk County, NY. He served as a Captain with the Morris County, N.J Militia in the Rev. Army from 1777 to 1778 and was said to have been a man of upstanding character.

He became known as Colonel Nathan when served as Colonel of the Regiment of the Militia for Ashe County, NC. In 1785 he and his wife Elizabeth and daughter Hannah left New Jersey for North Carolina, but Hannah died in Hagerstown, MD before the family could reach North Carolina. They first arrived near the Jersey Settlement in Rowan County, but moved to a farm near Holman's Ford in Wilks County. Soon they moved through Cook's Gap and settled on the New River, Wilks County (now Watauga) where Nathan acquired 600 acres in a state land grant. Nathan and Elizabeth were two of the original members of the Three Forks Baptist Church and are buried in the old church cemetery. Nathan, Jr. spent most of his fortune building a toll road from Cook's Gap to the Beaver Dams knows as Horton's turnpike. As an influential public servant he represented Ashe County in the House of Commons in 1800, 1801, and 1802 and in the NC Senate in 1805 and 1806."

"Wife of Nathan Horton (From the <u>Watauga Democrat</u>) "Rage of New York in 1786 to Figure in Watauga County's New Outdoor Play."

The rage of New York in 1763 probably never knew what she was getting into when she married Colonel Nathan Horton and settled in the Blue Ridge. She was Elizabeth Eagles, known to legend as the "Bell of Broadway" and the wilderness in which she created a home for her cavalier husband was right on the Indian frontier.

The story of the Hortons, and the brave people who joined then in blazing a westward train will be commemorated here this summer in an outdoor festival written by Kermit Hunter, who also wrote the Cherokee drama, "Unto These Hills." In that drama titled "Horn in the West" the newly organized Historical Association will depict the life story of Daniel Boone and the men and women who followed.

Elizabeth Eagles Horton who gave up fame for a far different existence is believed to be an ancestor of the more recent star of Broadway, Jeanne Eagles, who made a name for herself 150 years later in Summerset Mangham's "Rain."

The original "Belle of Broadway" was married to Colonel Horton in New York City, July 10, 1783. Three years later they settled in what was a century later to be called Watauga County—then only the New River section of Wilkes County.

The Colonel's choice of western North Carolina for a home made his first family strike out from the Atlantic Coast—but not the first to leave everything familiar behind him. The Hortons who live here now trace their ancestry back as far as 1100, to a hamlet in Buckinghammpshire in

England, which is 11 miles from London. The "Horton Church," built in that year still stands and still bears that name.

Descendants of the Revolutionary War, Colonel and his lady who still live in this section include Sam Horton, principal of Cove Creek School and former Watauga County Superintendent: and John Horton, who lives on part of the old home place. Records show that a third of the leading families of this section are related."

(2) Thomas Horton, Born 1602, Windsor in Mowsley, Leicestershire, England

(3) Jeremiah Jeremy Horton, Born April 1604, Mowsley, Lecs England

(4) Jeremiah Horton, Born April 1604, Mowsley, Leicestershire, England

(5) Joseph Horton 1606, Mowsley, Leicestershire, England

(6) Robert Ashley Horton, Born 1620, Springfield, Hampshire, MA, USA

Generation XV- William De Horton, Born 1550, Fifthouse, Halifax, England; Died 1640; Married Elizabeth Hanson, daughter of Thomas Hanson and Katherine Brooke, Halifax, Barkisland, Yorkshire, England; Born 1550-1552, Mowsley, Leicester, England; Children:

(1) Joseph Horton, Born about 1572, Mowsley, Leicester, England

(2) William Horton, Born about 1576, Barkisland, Yorkshire, England. Children: Thomas Horton was born in 1603 in Gumley, Leicestershire England to William and Isabella Horton and died October 1649 in Ireland. He was an English soldier in the Parliamentary army during the English Civil War. Though of humble background, he was taken under the wing of the powerful Sir Arthur Haselrig, and had become a

colonel by 1643. His troops played a decisive part in several important engagements, most notably the Battle of Naseby in 1645 and the Battle of St. Fagan's in 1648. As a reward for the valiant service her rendered for the cause, Horton was granted the confiscated lands of a deposed royalist. Thomas was a commissioner of the high court of justice in 1649, and thus was among those who signed the warrant for the execution of King Charles I of England. Later that year, he died of natural causes while serving with Cromwell in Ireland. His heirs were deprived of their estate at the Restoration. Gabriel, Born July 1, 1963

(3) Joshua Horton, ESQ, Born about 1577, Burksland, Halifax, York, England; Married Martha Binus

(4) Sarah Horton, Born about 1581, Burksland, Halifax, York, England; Married John Giedhill

(5) Elizabeth Horton, Born about 1583, Barkisland, Yorkshire, England

(6) Jeremiah Horton

Generation XVI- Barnabas De Horton, Born 1524, Leicestershire, England; Died 1570, Saddington, England; Married unknown Horton, Born 1530, Halifax, York, England, Marriage: 1549, Halifax, York, England; Children:

(1) William De Horton, Born 1550, Firthouse, Halifax, England

(2) John Horton, Born 1550

(3) William Horton, Born 1527, Mousley, Leichestershire, England

(4) Barnabas Horton, Born April 1540

(5) Jonathan Horton, Born 1552

Generation XVII- Richard De Horton, Born 1500, Mowsley, Leicestershire, England, Died 1483, Gloucheshire, England; Wife Ann Horton, Born 1450, Died 1515; Children:

(1) William Horton, Born 1476, Mosley, England

(2) Thomas De Horton, Born 1480, Mosley, England

(3) Richard De Horton, Born 1485, Mosley, England

(4) Joseph De Horton

(5) Barnabas De Horton, Born 1524, Leicestershire, England

Generation XVII- Richard De Horton, Born 1450, Mosley, Leicestershire, England; Died 1515; Wife Ann Horton, Born 1455, Leicestershire, England

(1) Thomas De Horton, Born 1480, Mowsley, England

Generation XIX- William De Horton, Born 1370, Mosley, Leicestershire, England; Died 1413; Wife: Joan De Dutton, Born: 1381, Hatton, Cheshire, England; Died: 1413; Marriage: 1405, Hatten, Chester, England; Children:

(1) Richard De Horton, Born 1399, Mowsley, Leicestershire, England,

(2) Margaret De Horton, Born: 1400, Horton, England

(3) Richard Horton, Born 1410, Mosley, Leicestershire, England.

Generation XX- John De Horton, Birth 1330, Knoptoff, Leicestershire, England, Death 1373, Wife, unknown Horton; Children:

(1) William De Horton, Born 1370, Mosley, Leicestershire, England

Generation XXI- Hugh De Horton, Birth 1300, Knoptoft, Leicester, England; Died 1333; Wife: Unknown Horton; Children:

(1) William De Horton, Born 1330, Knoptoft, Leicester, England

(2) John De Horton, Born 1330, Knoptoft, Leicester, England

(3) Henry De Horton, Born 1335, Knoptoft, Leicester, England

Generation XXII- Hugh De Wharton, (Horton) Born: 1270, Norton, Northampton- shire, England; Died: 1300; Wife unknown Horton; Children:

(1) William De Wharton (Horton)

(2) Nu De Horton, Birth 1296, Knoptoft, Leicester, England

(3) Hugh De Horton, Birth 1300, Knoptoft, Leicester, England

(4) John De Horton, Birth: 1330, Knoptoft, Leicester, England

Generation XXIII- Henry De Horton, Born, 1240, Horton, and Northampton, England: Died 1270; Children:

(1) Hugh De Wharton, Born 1270, Northampton shire, England

(2) Hugh De Horton, Born 1280

Generation XXIV- Hugh De Horton, Born 1220, Horton, Northampton, England, Died 1240; Wife: unknown Horton; Children:

(1) Henry De Horton, Born 1240, Horton, Northampton shire, England

Generation XXV- Robert De Horton, Born 1190, Horton, Northampton, England; Died 1220; Wife: unknown Horton; Children:

(1) Hugh De Horton, Born 1220, Horton, Northammpton, England

(2) Hugh De Orton Horton, Orton Cumberland, England

Generation XXVI- Hugh De Horton, Horton, Northampton, England; Wife unknown, children:

(1) Robert De Horton

Footnotes: Information taken from Mormon Records, Ancestor. com, Carroll County Records, Gilmer Horton, Sandra Llewellyn, Dean Brown, Jeanette Brown Martin,. Roots web.com, Maxine Grove, Wikepedia Encyclopedia, Winston Salem Journal, Watauga Democrat, Wytheville News; Family Bibles, Obituary records of Moody Funeral Home, Clara Chavier and James Horton, U. S. Census Records, and US Social Security Death Index.

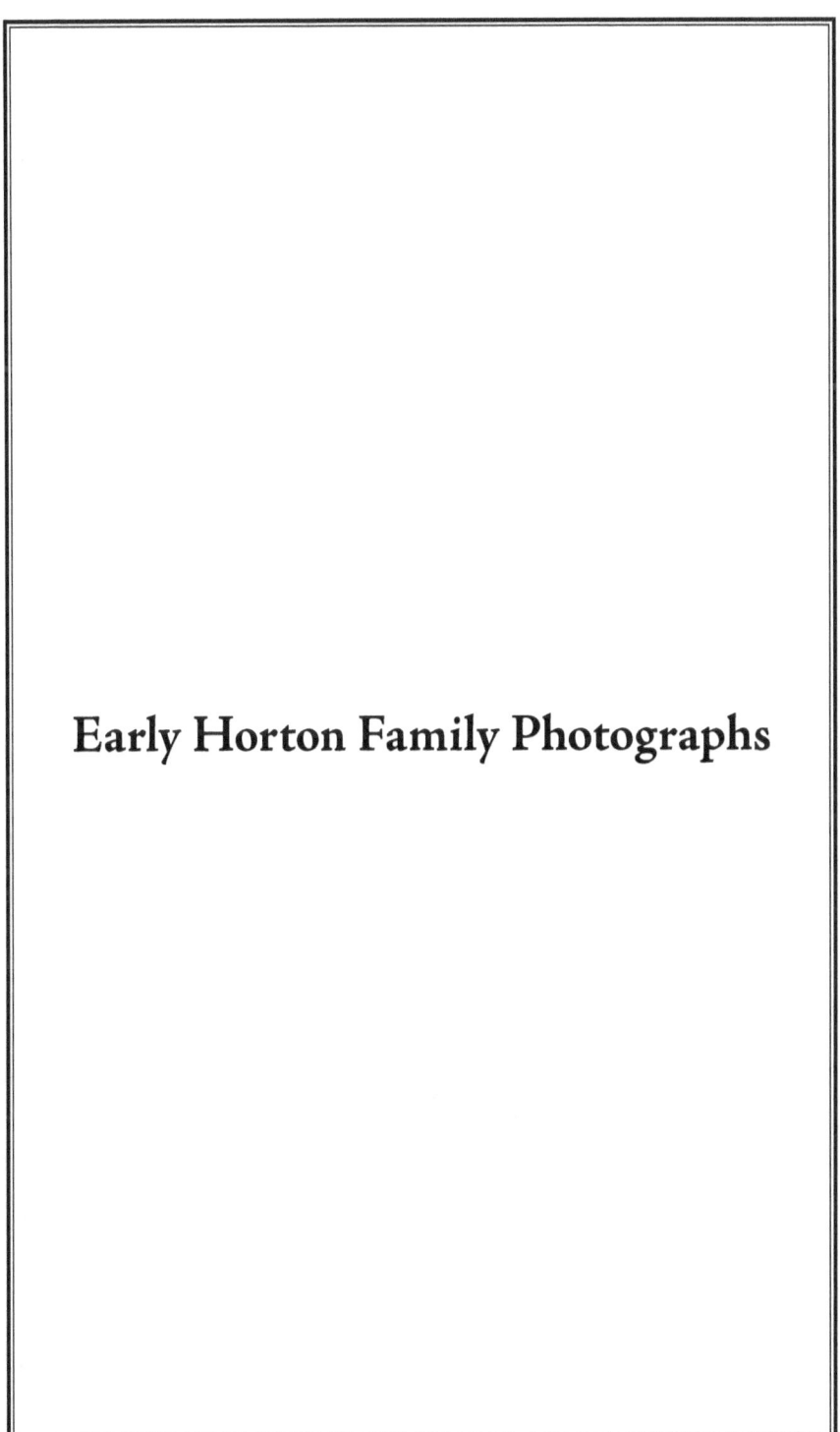

Early Horton Family Photographs

Annie Horton 1950   Marvin works in the Garden in the 50's

Horton Grandchildren, about 1940   Jean Horton about 1945

Helen and Arnold 1950   Gilmer Horton 1945

Ruth and Jean Horton

Dixie Norman, Dean Brown,
Dan Horton, 1942

The Children of MC and Annie Horton

Tommy Dara, Bud Goins, Arnold Draughon, Tom Brown,
Otis Chappell, Dean Brown, Mark Brown

Arnold Draughn in
Baltimore 1940's

Gilmer Horton at Christmas about 1957

Our DeHaven Family Crest

By Gilmer F. Horton

Famous DeHaven Ancestors!

Edwin Jessie DeHaven, Great, Great, Great Uncle. Born May 7, 1816 in Pennsylvania; Died May 1, 1865; (Edwin's great, great, grandfather Peter DeHaven was a brother to my g x 6 grandfather, Herman. Their father was Evert-1650) Grandfather, Explorer and Adventurer. He was appointed Acting Midshipman at the age of 10 and Passed Midshipman 5 years later. He Maine; sponsored by Miss H. N. De Haven, granddaughter of Lieutenant DeHaven; and commissioned 21 September 1942, Commander C. E. Tolman in command. He Surveyed Pacific, South American and Arctic waters. He commanded the first Grinnell Expedition to the Arctic in search of Sir John Franklin, and also to make scientific explorations. He was caught in the ice for nine months near Greenland and never managed to find Franklin. He had two US Naval Destroyers named after him. He is buried in Philadelphia, USAUSS DeHaven Launched Sunday from Iron Works (*from the Bath Daily Times, June 29, 1942*) Breaks Production Records at Big Shipyard Shattering still another production record, the USS DeHaven, sixth destroyer to be launched from Bath Iron Works Corp., in as many months, slipped quietly into the waters of the Kennebec, Sunday afternoon. It was the third Sunday launching in the history of the firm and the 47th ship of its type to be constructed here.

Several hundred spectators lined Carlton Bridge, many grouped on the Woolwich end to witness the spectacle but only a few were invited inside the yard. And many on the bridge did not see the ship until it was well out into the river for there were no whistles or clamor as she began to move slowly toward the river. Not until the bow had dropped from the ways did the two tugs assisting her salute with three blasts from their respective whistles.

Sponsoring the ship was Miss Helen N. DeHaven, Ardmore, Penn., a granddaughter of Lieut. Edwin Jesse DeHaven, USN, in whose honor the ship was named. Lieut. DeHaven, Commander of the Grinnell rescue expedition in 1950-51, failed in his attempt to rescue the explorer Sir John Franklin but discovered and named Grinnell Land while on the mission.

"Second Destroyer Named DeHaven is Launched Sunday"(Has Same Sponsor as First Ship of That Name) (*from the Bath Daily Times, January 10, 1944*)

The USS DeHaven; second destroyer bearing that name to be built at the Bath Iron Works Corp., was launched Sunday. Miss Helen N. DeHaven of Ardmore, Pa., who christened the first DeHaven in June 1942, also acted as sponsor of this ship, named for her grandfather, the late Lt. Edwin Jesse DeHaven. The first Bath built DeHaven was sunk in February of last year by Japanese air attack off Savo Island. The sponsor's party included Mrs. Richard Grosholz and her daughter, Virginia and Miss Edith Rolfe. Mrs. Grosholz and Miss Rolfe are also granddaughters of Lieut. DeHaven.

Samuel DeHaven, Killed 1858, Sdorus, IL.

In 1857, Thomas Patterson and his family moved to Sadorus, Illinois from Vermilion County, Illinois, to open a store. Being a newcomer to town, he was not very well liked. The following year, Samuel DeHaven, owner of a 160 acre farm near Sadorus, entered the store to buy a hatchet. DeHaven was popular in town, even thourh he was a bad tempered drunk. Patterson refused to sell DeHaven anything more on credit until his bill was paid. DeHaven, drunk, threatened Patterson with a spade, and Patterson defended himself by throwing a scale weight at DeHaven's head. DeHaven died of his head injuries a few hours later. Patterson was charged wit murder. He retained Abraham Lincoln and Leonard Swett as his attorneys. Patterson was found guilty of manslaughter and sentenced to three years in the new penitentiary in Joliet. He was pardoned after one year.

Related to Abraham Lincoln and Daniel Boone!

Thomas Lincoln (who married a DeHaven was the son of Abraham (Robeson) Lincoln and Anna Boone.

Anna Boone was the first cousin of the famous Daniel Boone.

Abraham Lincoln was the son of Mordecai Lincoln, Jr. who moved to Berks County in 1727. Mordecai had 11 children from two wives. Abraham was the youngest child and was born in 1736, the same year his father died. The oldest son of Mordecai was John Lincoln who moved to Linville's Creek, Virginia and later to Jefferson Co. Kentucky.

John Lincoln was the great grandfather of President Abraham Lincoln.

That's how the DeHaven family is related to President Abraham Lincoln as well as Daniel Boone.

Gloria DeHaven (born July 23, 1925, in Los Angeles, California) is an American actress.

The daughter of vaudeville performers, DeHaven began her career as a child actor as an extra in *Charlie Chaplin's Modern Times* (1936). She was signed to a contract with MGM

Studios and despite featured roles in such films as *The Thin Man Goes Home* (1945) she did not obtain the kind of stardom some had expected of her. In *Hollywood* (1976), she has guest starred in such television series as *Robert Montgomery Presents, The Rifleman, Wagon Train, Marcus Welby, M.D., Gunsmoke, Fantasy Island, Hart to Hart, The Love Boat, Highway to Heaven, Murder, She Wrote* and *Touched By An Angel.*

For her contribution to the motion picture industry, Gloria DeHaven has a star on the *Hollywood Walk of Fame* at 6933 Hollywood Blvd. She has also appeared as a regular in the television series and soap operas *As the World Turns, Mary Hartman* and *Ryan's Hope.* She was one of the numerous celebrities enticed to appear in the all-star box office.

David DeHaven was born in 1812 to Isaac DeHaven (born 1780, died 1856) and Hannah Miller (born 1781, died 1859 or 1869). David's grandfather was Harmon DeHaven (a blacksmith) of Lancaster, PA. David and Harmon, his brother, were successful businessmen. (Harmon was once mayor of Allegheny). David died on April 1, 1887.

Julia Lightner DeHaven was born on 1842 to David DeHaven and Eliza Wyke. Philip and Julia lived at one time at 65 Buena Vista Street, Allegheny, PA.

DeHavens Revolutionary War

Isaac DeHaven, Born February 16, 1750 in Loudoun County , Virginia. Great (x5) uncle; was a member of Captain Henry Lee's Company of Virginia Cavalry and was involved in several skirmishes near Philadelphia. He was discharged in December 1778. He was a corpal.

Abraham DeHaven, Born 1747, Loudon, Virginia; Great (x6) uncle fought in the Revolutionary War as a Private in for the Pennsylvania Troops.

Peter DeHaven, Born December 3, 1686, Mulheim, Westfalen, Germany; Great (x 8) uncle fought in the Revolutionary War as a Private for the Continental Troops.

Edward DeHaven, Born 1713, Great (x 9) uncle fought in the Revolutionary War as a Private for the Continental Troops.

John DeHaven, Born 1715, Great (x 9) uncle fought in the Revolutionary War as a Private for the Pennsylvania Troops.

Samuel DeHaven, Born 1746- 1821, fought in the Revolutionary War for the Pennsylvannia Troops. Great (x 9) uncle.

DeHaven Men of the Civil War

Isaac DeHaven, 51st Regiment of Pennsylvania Infantry of the Union Army and 4th Regiment of the PA Infantry of the Union Army.

Joseph DeHaven, 114th Regiment of the Pennsylvania Infantry of the Union Army.

John DeHaven, Union Infantry, 51st Regiment, Pennsylvania Infantry, 88th Regiment, Pennsylvania Infantry.

Isaac DeHaven, Born 1838, Private in Virginia Militia, Confederate Army.

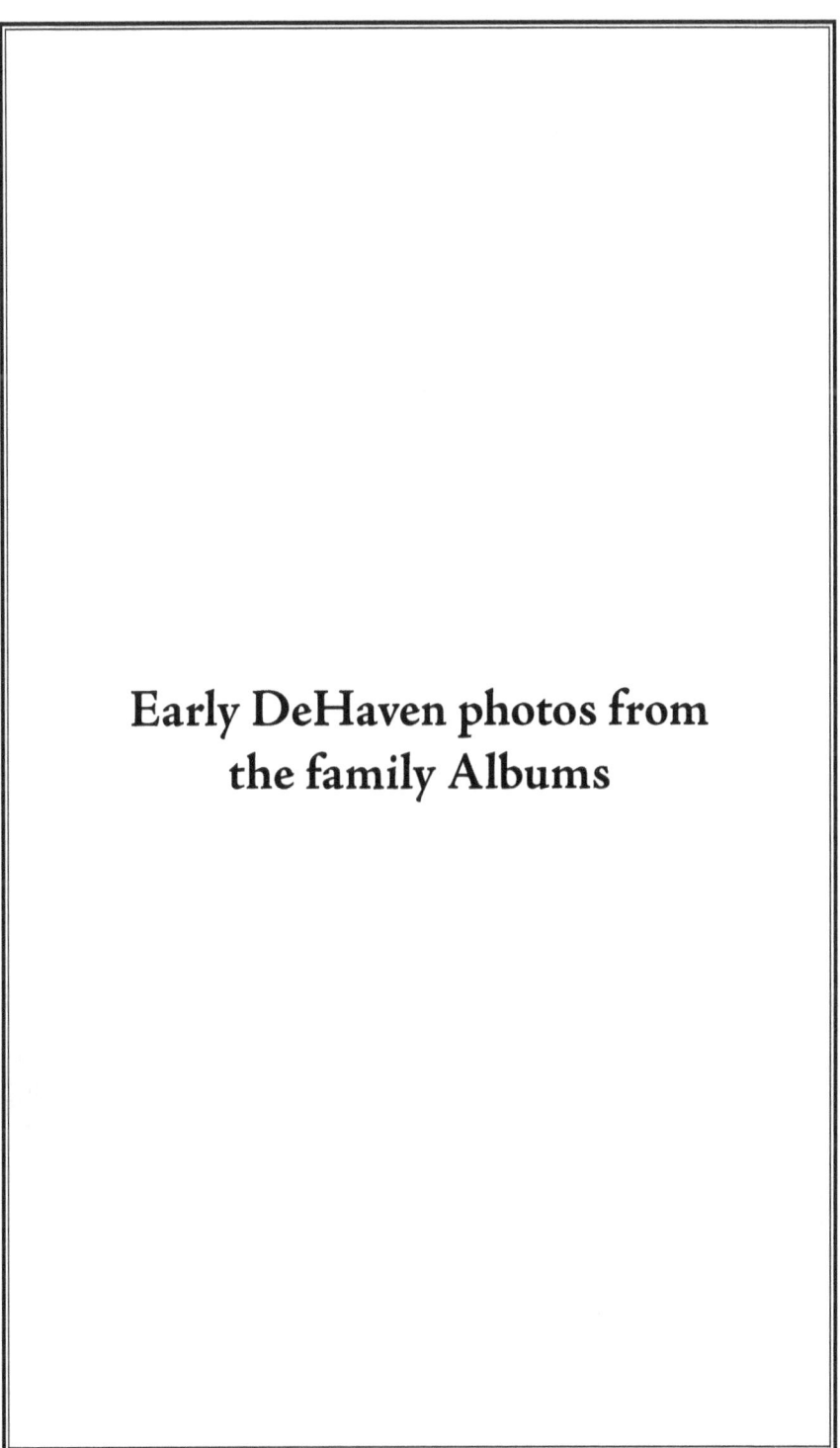

Early DeHaven photos from
the family Albums

Octavia DeHaven, Bill DeHaven, Lamie DeHaven Worrell
Lafay DeHaven, Leta DeHaven Garmon, Photo Made 1935.

DeHaven Brothers with their Mother Emaline DeHaven.

Elmer, Layfathe, Ray, Marvin, Arnold, Everett with their mother Octavia.

Emaline Bolt DeHaven, Wife of
William Marion DeHaven, and
Mother of Octavia DeHaven

Emaline Bolt DeHaven

William Marion DeHaven and
Grandson Marion Albert DeHaven

Octavia DeHaven

Rev. John Horton and Wife Tibitha

Genealogy of Our DeHaven Families

(Starting with the most recent generation and counting back)

Generation I- Dean Wayne Brown, Born 1938, Married Eleanor Bradley, Born 1937. Children:

(1) Mark Thomas Brown, Born 1966; Married: Shasta Bode, Born 1965, Date of Marriage: February 15, 1992; Children:

(a) Katherine Elizabeth Brown, Born, July 18, 1994;

(b) John-Henry Samuel Brown, Born, April 16, 1997

(2) Molly Elizabeth Brown, Born, October 8, 1969: Married: 1st, Robert Griffin, Born, October 8, 1970; Date of Marriage 1994; Children: Dominick Griffin, Born, December 24, 2002; 2nd Marriage, March 31, 2007, Robert Robinson, Born, August 30, 1973; One Son, Austin Robinson, Born May 20, 1995

Generation II- Katherine Florence Horton, Born June 28, 1920, Wythe, County, Virginia, Died October 5, 2004. The following is an account of her life, the way she told it. Her family moved to Mount Airy, NC, when she was eleven. She attended Franklin High School. At the age of seventeen, she fell in love and married Thomas Franklin Brown; they were married for 62 years, until his death. Katherine was a splendid mother and housekeeper. She spent her life looking after the needs of her three children: Dean Brown, Leon Brown, and

Jeanette Brown Chappell Martin. She had 10 grandchildren and 8 great grandchildren.

When she first married, she worked with her husband in their general store for a brief time, but later elected to stay home with her children. She loved to attend church and was a busy worker at the Mount Carmel Baptist Church where she taught Sunday school, sang in the choir, and was the WMU president. She loved her church work and her friends at Mount Carmel, and continued as long her health permitted. She once said she had a secret desire to play the piano as her daughter did, but was never able to achieve that life goal. After her husband retired they traveled together to Florida, several Southern states. She and her sisters Helen and Jean along with their mother traveled to California, a trip that Katherine spoke of until her death.

Katherine recalled the happiest times of her life were the children and grandchildren coming home for Christmas and getting ready for the event with her special cooking, and shopping. She was known for her Christmas cake recipes. Her Applesauce and Fresh Coconut Cakes were the envy of the City of Mount Airy and on occasions would sell some of them to special families.

Katherine credits her mother's strict teaching and guidance in making her the lady she turned out to be in life. She learned to work hard at a young age and to be respectful and polite to others. She said she had a wonderful life and doesn't regret anything. Married: Thomas Franklin Brown, Born 1919, Surry County, North Carolina; Children:

(1) Dean Wayne Brown, Born 1938, Married Eleanor Bradley, Born 1937, Date of Marriage December 27, 1964; Children:

(a) Mark Thomas Brown, Born 1966; Married: Shasta Bode, Date of Marriage: February 15, 1992. Children:

(1) Katherine Elizabeth Brown, Born 1994;

(2) John-Henry Samuel Brown, Born 1997

(b) Molly Elizabeth Brown, Born 1969: Married: 1ˢᵗ Robert Griffin, Date of Marriage 1994. Children: Dominick Griffin, Born 2002; 2ⁿᵈ Marriage, March 31, 2007, Robert Robinson, Born August 30, 1973, one son, Austin Robinson, Born May 20, 1995

(2) Roy Leon Brown, Born June 7, 1942; Married Janice Elaine Matthews, Born March 24, 1950; Married June 5, 1965; Children:

  (a) Karen Elaine Brown, Born December 5, 1967; Married 1ˢᵗ Keith Helton, 2ⁿᵈ Married John Barbe; Children:

    (1) Brittany Page Helton, Born March 20, 1984,

    (2) Brandy Nicolette Helton, Born November 6, 1990

  (b) Janice Susan Brown, Born December 5, 1969; Married: 1ˢᵗ Ronald Davis, 2ⁿᵈ Jeffery Bryson, 3ʳᵈ David Charles Utter; Children:

    (1) Julia Davis,

    (2) Megan Davis,

    (3) Living Son

  (c) Phillip Roy Brown

  (d) David Matthew Brown, Born December 5, 1973; Married July 9, 1971 to Jackie Lloyd, Born January 1, 1972; Children:

    (1) Carisia Danielle Brown, Born September 24, 2000;

    (2) Colby Matthew Brown, Born November 23, 2003

  (e) Michael Leon Brown, Born September 1, 1975; Married Lorraine Brown, Born November 23, 2003; Children:

    (1) Christian Michael Brown, Born May 13, 2000;

    (2) Caitlin Lorraine Brown, Born January 7, 2004

  (f) Timothy Gabriel Brown, Born March 25, 1982

(3) Jeanette Brown, Born June 16, 1945; Married 1st, Otis Chappell; Born March 20, 1943; Died February 13, 2003; Marriage, June 20, 1969, 2nd Clint Martin, May 13, 2007

   (a) Stephanie K. Chappell, Born November 11, 1970 Married David Warren McDuffie, Born February 15, 1968; Marriage September 13, 1997, Children:

      (1) Kathleen Clair (Katie) McDuffie, Born February 27, 2002:

      (2) Reece Tillman McDuffie, Born August 12, 2003

   (b) Julia Anna Chappell, Born August 17, 1973; Married James Stanley Marion, Born February 13, 1968; Marriage June 5, 1998; Children:

      (1) Anna Elizabeth Marion, Born September 30, 1999;

      (2) Meredith Craig Marion, Born January 9, 2002;

      (3) James Stanley Marion, Jr., Born December 7, 2004

Marvin and Annie Horton

Generation III- Marvin Chester Horton, Born January 24, 1897, Carroll County, VA.; Died 1964, Forsyth County, NC. Grandpa Horton was a tall heavy man, who probably weighed over 300 pounds.

Being tall, he carried his weight well. He had an accident when he was a young boy working with logs in the mountains and damaged his hip and legs. He had managed to recover without much medical attention but walked with a heavy limp and always used crutches. Sometimes he walked with one crutch and sometimes he used two crutches, according to how much pain he was feeling on that particular day. He suffered his entire life with severe pain from the logging accident. He spoke loudly with a deep voice and could be heard over anyone else that was talking. The corners of his mouth turned up in such a way that one would translate into a half-smile even when he was serious. He chewed Brown's Mule Tobacco and usually had some in his mouth with a few drops showing in the corners of his mouth. I always thought he was an intelligent man. He was open to new ideas and would become interested in anything new or ideas which I had to talk about. Once he ordered a donkey from Sears and Roebuck bought a camera and tried making pictures of children at events. He had no way to haul the donkey except in the back seat of his car, which he had won at a drawing at the Surry County Fair. It was a funny sight to see him driving down the road with the donkey looking out the back seat window. He had a love for dogs, horses, friends and telling tall tales. Married: Annie Myrtle Surratt, Born 1897; Died 1982; Children:

(1) Gilmer Fred Horton, Ret. T-Sergeant, US Air Force, Born 1917; Died 1982. Gilmer graduated from Franklin High School in Surry County and entered Mount Airy High School the next year. The principal at Mount Airy wanted to know why he wanted two diplomas.

After Gilmer explained that he needed Latin, Physics, Chemistry, Algebra, mechanical drawing and some other important courses that he had not received at his previous High School, he was permitted to enter and did receive a diploma from Mount Airy High School in 1938. During this period of time Gilmer pursued a career with the US Department of

Justice. There is a copy of a letter from J. Edgar Hoover related to this inquiry. In 1953 he was discharged from the US Air Force.

Gilmer's most significant assignment during that service was listed as Hq. 98ᵗʰ Bomb Wing (SAC). He served in France, Tunisian and Sicilian campaign. He was Mount Airy's first volunteer. His medals and commendations included: Good Conduct Medal w/2 Loops, National Defense Service Medal, Commendation Ribbon w/Metal Pendant, Korean Service Medal, and United Nations Service Medal. He received a Military Training Certificate from Fort Bragg in Field Artillery. After his discharge in 1945, he reentered the US Army and was assigned to the Intelligence division in the United Kingdom where he earned the World War II Victory Medal. His next service was with the United States Air Force, earning the Army of Occupational Medal, American Defense Medal, Good Conduct Medal, EAME Campaign Medal, and the American Thea Medal. Not much is known about the intelligence work; however it is known that it carried him all over the world.

One document reads: "Assisted in the collection evaluation interpretation and distribution of information of enemy and counter-intelligence activities and the safe guarding of military information." There is a personal note from Harry S. Truman, commending him on his performance. Another citation from the 9ᵗʰ Infantry Division states the following: "On the night of the 14ᵗʰ of August, 1943, in the City of Cesaro, Sicily, awakened by explosions and resultant fire from an enemy bombing attack, and fire of the ammunition dump at the AMGOT Headquarters and the building housing the public records of the country. Gilmer immediately seized the initiative and by valorous and aggressive efforts extinguished the flames, thereby eliminating a possible disaster. His performance, at great risk to his own safety, merits high commendations".

He was an inventor and is credited with an invention of a fuel valve that regulated the flow of fuel in jet engines. This invention was adapted by Canada, United Kingdom, and France, but was never used in the

USA. Gilmer enjoyed doing research, and is credited with designing several medals for the US Air Force.

Gilmer loved his family and especially nephews and nieces. He always drew his own Christmas Cards which he sent to us. He never married, however, I do know of several loves he had before and after he retired in his later years. He loved guns, and always carried one for protection along with two rottweiler dogs, even when he took his daily strolls in the woods. After his death, even though the dogs knew me very well and were friendly toward me, they would not let me in the house, and I had to pay to have them "done away with" before I could enter the house.

He loved to travel back to his home place in Max Meadows; he and I made that trip many times. He always kept a daily journal and that collection can be seen at the Mount Airy Museum of Regional History, in Mount Airy, NC. Gilmer died of cancer May 7, 1982, and was buried at Oakdale Cemetery, Mount Airy, NC.

(2) Ruth Horton, Born 1918; Died May 4, 1988; Married Buddy Isaac Goings, Born August 7, 1920; Died March 4, 2005; Children:

(a) Sandra Ann Goings, Born June 23, 1950

(3) Katherine Horton, Born June 28, 1920; Died October 5, 2004; Married Thomas Franklin Brown; Died October 3, 1999; Children:

(a) Dean Wayne Brown, Born November 26, 1938,

(b) Roy Leon Brown, Born June 7, 1942,

(c) Ann Jeanette Brown Chappell Martin, Born June 16, 1945; (Detailed Information above)

(4) Helen Horton, Born July 15, 1922, Died February 28, 2008; Married Arnold V. Draughn; Born January 29, 1920, Died May 15, 1960

(5) Mazie Goldie Horton, Born March, 2, 1924, Died March 2007, Married Tommy Dara; Born July 16, 1910; Died August 23, 1985, Vero Beach, Florida; Children:

    (a) Deborah Ann Dara, Born April 1, 1951, Children: 1 daughter; Makenzie Alma Dara, Born November 30, 2001

    (b) Steven Dara, Born March 10, 1955

(6) Daniel C. Horton, Born October 10, 1926; Wythe County, Virginia; Died January 5, 1992, Miami, Florida; Married Frances Horton; Died July 2006; Children:

    (a) Daniel Chester Horton, Born January 23, 1950, Married Elizabeth Frances Rubis;

    (b) Kenneth Michael Horton, Born November 7, 1955,

    (c) Richard Francis Horton, Born April 6, 1961.

(7) Jean Horton, Born June 8, 1932; Married (Gus) Ural Sigmon Gabriel; Born 1928; Died August 8, 1990; Children:

    (a) Scott Alan Gabriel, Born, January 15, 1961, Children: Zachary Aaron Gabriel, Born November 19, 1990 and Jacob Alan Gabriel, Born February 19, 1994;

    (b) Bryan Phillip Gabriel, Born July 1, 1963

Generation IV- Octavia DeHaven, Born April 29, 1870, Carroll County, Virginia; Died June 19, 1959, Carroll, Virginia. Married Michael Marvin Horton, Born January 27, 1875; Died July 28, 1934 Great Grandpa and Great Grandmother DeHaven were managers of Max Meadows General Store. Children:

(1) Rupert Everett Horton, Born March 23, 1895, Died 1967; Wife: Elizabeth Midkiff Horton, Born September, 13, 1898, Died July 21, 1996; Children: (See Horton Genealogy)

(a) Virginia Pauline Horton, Born August 5, 1922, Surry County; Died 1924 (See Horton Genealogy)

(b) Marie Horton Lawrence, Born 1920, Died September 14, 2004, Southern Pines, NC (See Horton Genealogy)

(c) Sadie Bell Horton Spargo, Born October 24, 1939 (See Horton Genealogy)

(d) Rupert Clarence Horton, Born August 23, 1926; (See Horton Genealogy)

(e) Clara Horton, Born April 2, 1930; Married (Joe) Joseph Chavier, Born September 27, 1920, Mass. Died February 9, 2007 (See Horton Genealogy)

(f) James Clifford Horton, Born 1937, Married Carol Johnson, Born October 24, 1939; Children:

    (1) Joseph Anthon; Horton, (Joey),

    (2) William Jefferson Horton (Jeff),

    (3) James Clifford Horton, Jr. (Jamey,

(2) Marvin Chester Horton, Born 1897; Died 1964; Married: Annie Myrtle Surratt; Children:

    (a) Gilmer Horton,

    (b) Ruth Horton,

    (c) Katherine Horton,

    (d) Helen Horton,

    (e) Mazie Horton,

    (f) Daniel Horton,

    (g) Jean Horton (See Horton Genealogy)

(3) Pearl Telipha Horton; Born April 26, 1914; Died 1994; Married Charles Brown; Children:

(a) June Brown (See Horton Genealogy)

(4) Elmer Elis Horton, Born December 9, 1915; Died August 3, 1984. Children: Elmer E. Horton of Richmond, Virginia; Children:

(a) Elmer E. Horton, Jr. (See Horton Genealogy)

(5) Wilford Arnold Horton, Born June 6, 1905; Died March 5, 1973; Married Bessie V. Horton, Born 1903; Died 1993, Children:

(a) Orbra C. Horton, Born 1927, Pulaski, Virginia. Children:

(1) Clinton Horton,

(2) Minnie Horton,

(3) Owen Horton,

(4) Thelma Horton,

(5) Bob Horton,

(6) Myrtle Horton,

(7) Richard Horton (See Horton Genealogy)

(6) Susan Leanona Horton Groves, Born June 6, 1903; Died 199;. Married Robert W. Groves, Born 1896; Died 1974; Children:

(a) Edwin Groves,

(b) Bobby Groves (See Horton Genealogy)

(7) Early Raymond Horton (Ray), Born 1911; Children:

(a) Don Horton,

(b) Joyce Horton,

(c) Julian Horton (See Horton Genealogy)

(8) George Lafayette (Fate) Horton; Children:

(a) William Horton,

(b) Dewey Horton,

(c) Christine Horton (See Horton Genealogy)

(9) Daisy Lee Horton, Born 1912, Died April 20, 1914

(10) May Horton; Children:

(a) Thomas Mabry, Jr.

Generation V- William Marion DeHaven, Born October 28, 1846, Virginia; Died March 12, 1929, Carroll County, Virginia; Married Emaline A. Bolt, Born Jan. 9, 1842, Carroll County, Virginia; Died Nov. 19, 1917, Carroll County, Virginia; Children:

(1) Sarah Alice DeHaven, Born November 8, 1864, Hillsville, Carroll, Virginia

(2) Lewis Masterson DeHaven, Born October 26, 1866, Carroll, Virginia

(3) Flurnoy E. Dehaven, Born October 3,

(4) Octavia DeHaven, Born April 29, 1870, Carroll County, Virginia; Died June 19, 1959, Carroll, Virginia

(5) Letitia Ellen Dehaven, Born January 26, 1872

(6) Edward Lafayette DeHaven, Born Feb. 1847; Died 1961

(7) William Thomas DeHaven, Born May 29, 1876, Carroll County, Virginia; Died 1959; Wife Zella Grace Fariss

(8) Harrison Powell DeHaven, Born March 12, 1879, Virginia

(9) Lucy Ann DeHaven, Born June 19, 1881, Carroll County, Virginia

(10)   Solomon Oscar DeHaven, Born August 1883

(11)   Daniel DeHaven, Born March 16, 1887

Generation VI- Abraham DeHaven, Born 1794; Died 1879; Wife Mary Ann Chitwood, Born May 10, 1804; Died Jan. 4, 1882; Marriage January 4, 1820; Children:

(1)   Martha DeHaven, Born October 1, 1820, Virginia

(2)   Joseph DeHaven, Born 1823, Carroll County, VA

(3)   James Madison DeHaven, Born 1825, Carroll County, Va.; Died 1905. Wife, Martha Hale, Born 1830; Married December 15, 1852. Children:

    (a)   Mary DeHaven, Born 1853,

    (b)   Lousia DeHaven, Born 1857,

    (c)   Wesley DeHaven, Born 1861,

    (d)   Washington Columbus DeHaven, Born 1863, Morgan Co., Kentucky;

    (e)   Lucenda DeHaven, Born 1865;

    (f)   Calvin DeHaven, Born 1867

(4)   Hannah DeHaven, Born 1827

(5)   Salome DeHaven, Born 1829, Franklin County, Va.; Married Harrison Cox, May 7, 1849 in Carroll County Virginia.

(6)   George Washington DeHaven, Born 1830

(7)   Jessie DeHaven, Born 1834, Carroll County, Va

(8)   Polly DeHaven, Born 1836

(9)   Mary Ann DeHaven, Born 1837 Grayson/Carroll County, Va.; Died June 16, 1916, Carroll County, Va.; Married Newell McHome in Carroll County, 1861

(10) Lewis DeHaven, Born 1837

(11) John DeHaven, Born 1838, Grayson/Carroll County, VA

(12) Margaret DeHaven, Born 1838

(13) Abraham Wesley DeHaven, Born 1840, Grayson/Carroll County, VA; Married Eliza Jane Lundy.

(14) Drucilla DeHaven, Born 1842, Carroll County VA.; Died October 7, 1894, Carroll County Virginia.

(15) Isaac Washington DeHaven, Born 1845, Carroll County, VA; Died November 23, 1864, White Sulphur Springs, Greenbrier County, West VA Isaac was a Private in the CSA War for the Virginia Militia. He joined when he was 14 years old and on his way to training camp caught pneumonia and died.

(16) William Marion DeHaven, Born 1846, Carroll County, VA; Died March 12, 1929; Married Emmaline Americ Bolt; Born January 9, 1842; Died November 19, 1917

(17) Squire Anderson DeHaven, Born March 4, 1851, Carroll County, Va; Died July 14, 1909; Carroll County, Va.; Married Columbia Fleming, Born Sept. 23, 1849; Died January 29, 1919, Carroll County, Va

Generation VII- Jessie DeHaven, Born 1759, Philadelphia, PA; Died 1843, Grayson County, VA; Married Drucilla (?), Died 1840, Grayson County, VA; Children:

(1) Mary DeHaven

(2) James DeHaven, Born 1789, Virginia

(3) Nancy DeHaven, Born 1791

(4) Abraham DeHaven, Born August 28, 1794, Franklin, Virginia

(5) Martha Ann DeHaven, Born August 13, 1796, Grayson, Virginia

(a) Martha DeHaven, Born 1820, Franklin County, VA; Died March 1, 1900, Carroll County, VA; Married Archibald Akers; Born October 5, 1820, Montgomery/Floyd County, VA; Died January 25, 1898; Married January 25, 1847, Carroll County VA; Children: 9 children.

Loudoun County, Virginia Will Books, Will Book A. "Will of Abraham Dehaven, Loudoun Co., VA, dated 13 Sept. 1770 Proved: on oaths of George McKenney, Elias Ellis, and William DeHaven.

Wife: Robetta - my new house and 1 acre of land it stands on, situated at the great road leading from Noland's ferry to Leesburg with 20 acres joining house on the south side of road during her life.

Sons: Jesse - 20 acres at wife's decease

Jacob - residue of land on south side

Abraham & Isaac - land on north side of road

Daus: Robetta & Sarah – each to have a horse or mare of 12L value, feather bed 6 pewter plates, two dishes, bason, spinning whel, saddle of 4:10 Pennsylvania currency value; sows, cow, etc...to be paid out of the estate on north side of road by Abraham and Isaac. Robetta's to be paid within two years. The daughters are to have maintenance with Abraham and Isaac until they marry or remove; to work for use of family as long as they remain with their brothers.

Elizabeth - horse, saddle of equal value with her sisters, pewter,...paid when she is 18 years old, to be paid by Jacob.

Jesse (son) and Elizabeth to each get a years schooling out of estate

Daughter Hannah - one shilling, she being fully provided for.

Daughter Ann - one shilling, she being already provided for

Executors: wife Robetta, sons Abraham and Isaac

Witnesses: George McKinney, Elias Ellis, William DeHaven

Securities: Isaac DeHaven, Henry Oxley, Jr., Shadrach Samuels, and Elias Ellis

(6) Jessie DeHaven, Born 1798, Franklin, Virginia

(7) Drucilla DeHaven, Born 1805, Franklin, Virginia

(8) Harriet DeHaven, Born March 9, 1804, Scott, Kentucky

(9) Tillitha Cuma DeHaven, Born January 7, 1805, Scott, Kentucky

(10) Tabitha DeHaven, Born March 1805

(11) Elizabeth DeHaven, Born 1808, Scott, Kentucky

(12) Samuel DeHaven, Born 1811, Scott, Kentucky

(13) Mahala DeHaven, Born 1812, Scott, Kentucky

(14) Jacob DeHaven, Born January 18, 1813, Scott, Kentucky

(15) Alemeda DeHaven, Born 1817, Scott, Kentucky

(16) Permelia DeHaven, Born 1818, Scott, Kentucky

Generation VIII- Abraham DeHaven, 1714, Skippack, Philadelphia, Pennsylvania; Died 1771 Leesburg, Loudoen, Virginia; Married, Rebecca Pauling, Born 1716, Died March 3, 1776, Leesburg, Loudoen, Virginia; Married 1736, Montgomery, Virginia; Children:

(1) Hannah DeHaven, Born 1734, Philadelphia

(2) Ann DeHaven, Born 1741, Philadelphia

(3) Abraham DeHaven, Born 1747, Loudon, Virginia; Abraham fought in the American Revolunitary War as a Private for the Pennsylvania Troops.

(4) Isaac DeHaven, Born 1750, Providence, Philadelphia

(5) Jacob DeHaven, Born 1750, Montgomery, Pennsylvania

(6) Elizabeth DeHaven, Born December 29, 1737, Philadelphia

(7) Mary DeHaven, Born 1741, Philadelphia

(8) Sarah DeHaven, Born 1753, Philadelphia

(9) Rebecca DeHaven, Born 1754, Philadelphia

(10) Jessie DeHaven, Born 1759, Philadelphia

Generation IX- Herman DeHaven (Herman In Den Hoffen), Born July, 1682, Died March, 1753; Married Ameken DeGref (Annid Op DeHaven); Born 1684, Died 1726; Children

(1) Edward DeHaven, Born 1713; Edward fought in the American Rev. War as a Private for the Continental Troops.

(2) Abraham DeHaven, Born 1714

(3) John DeHaven, Born 1715; John fought in the American Rev. War as a Private for the Pennsylvania, Troops.

(4) Katherine DeHaven

(5) Elizabeth DeHaven

(6) Mary DeHaven

(7) Margaret DeHaven

(8) Harmond DeHaven, 1729; Harmond Dehaven had a son named Edward Dehaven. Edward's daughter was named Alice Dehaven; Alice married Thomas Lincoln who was Abraham Lincoln's Grandfather. Thomas Lincoln had a father named Abraham Lincoln who married Ana Boone. Ana Boone was the Daughter of Jessie Boone; the granddaughter of Israel Boone and the Son of Squire Boone who was the father of Daniel Boone. This makes Abraham Lincoln and Daniel Boone our distant cousins.

(9) Issac DeHaven, Born 1731

(10) Jacob DeHaven,

There is also no evidence to support the claim of the DeHaven family that their ancestor Jacob DeHaven lent George Washington $450,000 in cash and supplies while the army was encamped at Valley Forge. This tradition first appeared in print in a history of the DeHaven family penned by Howard DeHaven Ross. Periodically, the descendants of Jacob DeHaven make attempts to get the "loan" repaid with interest. Various individuals took up this cause in the 1850s, 1870s, and 1890s. The issue came up again around 1910, 1920, and 1960. As recently as 1990, the New York Times reported on the status of a class action suit filed in U.S. Claims Court by a DeHaven descendant from Stafford, Texas. The DeHavens calculated the amount owed their family at more than one hundred billion dollars, but they reported they were willing to accept a "reasonable payment" — and maybe a monument at Valley Forge. This remarkably persistent tradition has been thoroughly debunked by Judith A. Meier, of the Historical Society of Montgomery County, whose genealogical research revealed that there were no DeHavens living in the immediate area until after 1790 and that Jacob DeHaven had never been rich enough to make such a fabulous loan. Still, past experience shows that a DeHaven claim is certain to arise about once every generation

Generation X- Everett DeHaven, Born 1650, Mulheim, Germany; Died March 4, 1728, Philadelphia, PA; Married Elizabeth Shipbower, Born 1650; Died, 1728, Whitepain, Philadelphia, PA; Marriage May 21, 1674, Evangelical Reform Church, Mulheim, Westphalla, Germany; Children:

(1) William DeHaven, Born 1680

(2) Wilheilm DeHaven, Born November 29, 1680, Mulheim, Westphalla, Germany

(3) Gerhard DeHaven, Born May 12, 1681, Mulheim, Westphalla, Germany

(4) Herman Harmon DeHaven, Born 1682, Mulheim, Prussia

(5) Peter DeHaven, Born December 3, 1686, Mulheim, Westfalen, Germany

(6) Annere Anna DeHaven, Born 1691

Generation XI- Theis In Hoffen, Born 1645: Married Anna Gerdraud; Children:

(1) Evert In De AHaven, 1650

(2) Wilhelm In De Hoffen, 1650

(3) Wilhelm In Hoffen, 1650

(4) Peter In Hoffen, 1655

Gen-eration XII- Wilhelm in de haven; Wife: Aufon Kompefe, Married in Mulheim, Germany 1625.

Footnotes: Information taken from Mormon Records, Ancestor. com, Carroll County Records, Gilmer Horton, Sandra Llewellyn, Dean Brown, Jeanette Brown Martin,. Roots web.com, Maxine Grove, Wikepedia Encyclopedia, Winston Salem Journal, Watauga Democrat, Wytheville News; Family Bibles, Obituary records of Moody Funeral Home, Clara Chavier and James Horton, U. S. Census Records, and US Social Security Death Index.

Four Generations, Octavia, Marvin, Katherine, Jeanette

M. M. Horton and his horse Raymond

Surratt Coat of Arms, By Gilmer Horton

History of Our Surratt Family

(Starting with the most recent generations and counting back)

Generation I- Dean Wayne Brown, Born 1938, Married December 27, 1964 to Eleanor Bradley, Born January 30, 1937; Children:

(1) Mark Thomas Brown, Born August 4, 1966; Married: Shasta Bode, Born July 3, 1965, Date of Marriage 1992; Children:

    (a) Katherine Elizabeth Brown, Born July 18, 1994;

    (b) John-Henry Samuel Brown, Born April 16, 1997

(2) Molly Elizabeth Brown Robinson, Born October 8, 1969: 1st Married: Robert Griffin, Born October 8, 1970, Date of Marriage July 2, 1994; Children: Dominick Griffin, Born December 24, 2002; 2nd Marriage, March 31, 2007, Robert Robinson, Born August 30, 1973; Children:

    (a) Austin Robinson, Born May 20, 1995

Generation II- Katherine Florence Horton, Born June 28, 1920, Wythe, County, Virginia, Died October 5, 2004 Married: Thomas Franklin

Brown, Born 1919, Died October 2001, Surry County, North Carolina; Children:

(1) Dean Wayne Brown, Born November 26, 1938, Married Eleanor Crain Bradley, Born January 30, 1937, Date of marriage, December 27, 1964; Children:

(a) Mark Thomas Brown, Born August 4, 1966;

(b) Molly Elizabeth Brown, Born October 8, 1969 (see Horton Genealogy for More details)

(2) Roy Leon Brown, Born June 7, 1942 Married Janice Matthews, Born March 24, 1950; Date of Marriage: June 5, 1965, Children:

(a) Karen Brown,

(b) Janice Susan Brown,

(c) David Brown,

(d) Michael Brown,

(e) Phillip Brown,

(f) Timothy Brown. (see Horton Genealogy for more details)

(3) Jeanette Brown Martin, Born June 16, 1945; 1st Married Otis Chappell, June 22, 1969; He was Born March 20, 1943, Died February 13, 2003; Children:

(a) Stephanie Chappell, Born November 21, 1970

(b) Julie Chappell, Born August 17, 1973. 2nd Marriage Clinton Franklin Martin, May 6, 2007 (see Horton Genealogy for more details)

Generation III- Annie Myrtle Surratt Horton, Born January 29, 1897, Carroll County, Virginia, Died February 25, 1982, Surry County, NC

Married Marvin Chester Horton, Born, 1897; Virginia, Died January 24, 1969, Forsyth County, NC; Children:

(1) Gilmer Horton, Born 1916,

(2) Ruth Horton, Born 1918,

(3) Katherine Horton, Born 1920,

(4) Helen Horton, Born 1922,

(5) Mazie Goldie Horton, Born 1924,

(6) Daniel Horton, Born 1927,

(7) Jean Horton Born 1932,

(8) Leonard Horton,Born 1935, *(Leonard lived one day) (See Horton Genealogy for more details.)*

Grandma Horton was a kind, loving mother and grandmother. She was always interested in her children and proud of all of them. She was a humble lady who worked hard at home, growing her flowers, a large garden, canning vegetables and fruit. She always picked wild berries and made jelly and jam. She raised her own chickens for eggs and food.

Her fried chicken was always a treat; however, she never had the heart to eat one herself. She had a cow, which a neighbor allowed her to keep in his pasture, and made her own butter from a hand churn. She grew grapes and made jelly and jams from them. She fell from a chair while picking grapes and broke her hip, which eventually caused her to be sent to a nursing home. Grandma was a wonderful quilt maker and made many beautiful quilts alone.

She also worked with several ladies of the community making quilts. They would often sit around the large quilting frame and as they sewed, they would tell tales about different things that had happened in their lives. I was the oldest grandchild and remember many things she taught me as a child. She attended Mount Carmel Baptist Church regularly and sat in the "A-Men Corner". She loved to sing hymns, when she was alone, in a high falsetto voice, which I still remember after 50 years. She cooked on a wood stove, made her own soap in a large pot in the yard. She raised her own hog, and each fall when the weather turned cold, we would kill the hog and process the meat making sausage, curing the hams and shoulders. She always made "chitlens," canned the sausage, and pickled the feet for grandpa to enjoy. She always gave away the head and other parts to needy neighbors. Grandma slept on a straw tick, which is a homemade mattress made of straw. One of her spring cleaning rituals was to throw away the old straw and find new clean straw and stuff the mattress. I shall always remember her old fashioned ways and the "half-smile" she would show when she approved of something the grandchildren had done.

Generation IV- James Surratt, Born in Virginia, Died in Virginia. James was born and raised near Carroll County, Virginia. He was a High School Graduate and worked for the Railroad as an accountant. He is buried along the banks of the New River at Foster Falls, Virginia. Married, Mickie Ann Fitzgerald, Born in Virginia, Died in Virginia. Children:

(1) Annie Myrtle, Born January 29, 1897; Married Marvin C. Horton January 28, 1916; Died February 25, 1982, Surry County, NC.

Grandmother gives the following account in an oral history interview when she was in her late 70's: "My mother was a loving, kind person, she loved all her children. When I was a child at the age of three she had health problems and 'went crazy.' All the younger children were sent to separate homes." When I asked if her childhood was happy, she replied, "we were as happy as children could be, as we were cared for, given warm clothing, food, and a safe place to stay, I don't regret it." A check of the 1910 and 1920 Mormon Census Records does indeed reveal that as a child of three and later age 13 she was living in a home where she was not related; Children:

(a) Gilmer Fred Horton, Born January 15, 1917, Died May 7, 1982; Never Married (see Horton Genealogy)

(b) Ruth Almer Horton, Born July 12, 1918; Married Buddy Issac Goins August 9, 1944; Children:

   (1) Sandra Ann Goins, Married Larry Thomas Llewellyn, April 4, 1979 (see Horton Genealogy)

(c) Katherine Florence Horton, Born June 28, 1920; Married Thomas Franklin Brown July 11, 1937; Children:

   (1) Dean Wayne Brown, Married Eleanor Crain Bradley, December 27, 1964,

   (2) Roy Leon Brown Married Janice Mathews, June 5, 1965,

   (3) Ann Jeanette Brown, Married Otis Chappell, Jr. 1st, June 22, 1969 Clinton Martin 2nd; (see Horton Genealogy)

(d) Helen Aleen Horton, Born July 15, 1922, Died February 28, 2008; Married Arnold Draughn August 9, 1944; No Children (see Horton Genealogy)

(e) Mazie Golden Horton, Born March 2, 1924; Married Tommy Dara March 11 about 1945; Children:

   (1) Deborah Ann Dara, Married Hank Pohl, August 2, 1975, daughter Makenzie Alma Dara, Born November 30, 2001

   (2) Steven Dara (see Horton Genealogy)

(f) Daniel Chester Horton, Born October 10, 1927; Married Frances Theresa Reiss, April 2, 1949; Children:

   (1) Daniel Chester Horton, Jr., Married Elizabeth Frances Rubin, December 12, 1976

(2) Kenneth Michael Horton,

(3) Richard Francis Horton (see Horton Genealogy)

(g) Jean Ellen Horton, Born June 8, 1932; Married Ulysis Sigmon Gabriel April 17, 1954; Children:

(1) Scot Alan Gabriel,

(2) Bryan Phillip Gabriel (see Horton Genealogy)

(h) Leonard Horton, Born January 24, 1935, Died January 24, 1935

(2) Joseph Monsey Surratt; Married Elizabeth_____; Children: Joseph Died at the age of 59. He was a train engineer.

(3) Martha Ann Surratt; Died in infancy

(4) Samuel Surratt, Died in infancy

(5) Elizabeth Surratt, Born March 23, 1894; Married Arville Charles Austin; Children:

(a) Clara Virginia Austin, Born November 10, 1916; Married Ford McConnell

(b) Dorcus Louise Austin, Born June 11, 1919; Married Lewis Roseberry; Children Jan Teresa Roseberry, Married Jeffery Butcher

(c) Fred Swanson Austin, Born February 14, 1923, Died 1948, Never Married

(d) Joseph Warren Austin, Born December 21, 1920; Married Alice Cooper; Children Mary Jane Austin; Married Donnell Duncan; Children Todd Duncan

(e) Ray Rudolph Austin, Born December 25, 1924; Married Betty Fretwell

(f) Herbert Wayne Austin, February 9, 1931; Never Married

(g) Carl Austin, February 14, 1928; Never Married

(6) Guy Posey Surratt, never married.

(7) Arthur French Surratt; Married Edna Bell Stone; Born June 28, 1893; Died March 17, 1954; *Arthur Died at the age of 62.* Children:

   (a) Trent Surratt

   (b) Esther Surratt; Never married

   (c) Robert Surratt

   (d) James Surratt

   (e) Kelly Surratt

   (f) Mary Surratt

   (g) Beulah Surratt; Never Married

Generation V- Uriah Surratt, Born 1855, Virginia; Married Perlina Peak, Virginia; Wife Perlina Peak, Born 1846, Died 1847. Uriah's unit fought at First Manassas under General Cocke, then was assigned to General Picketts, Garnetts, and Huntons's Brigade. He participated in the campaigns of the Army of Northern Virginia from Williamsburg to Gettysburg. He later served in North Carolina, returned to Virginia and took an active part in the battles of Drewry's Bluff and Cold Harbor. The 18th endured the hardships of the Petersburg trenches north of the James River and saw action around Appomattox. Children;

(1) James A. Surratt, Born 1877

(2) Sally A. Surratt, Born 1878

(3) Cora A Surratt, Born 1880

(4) James William Surratt, Born 1881;

(5) David Anderson Surratt

(6) Laura T. Surratt, 1887

Generation VI- James Alfred Surratt, Born 1832, Grayson County, Virginia; Died 1863, Rock Island, Illinois. Married: Useley, Born 1832, Grayson County, Virginia; Died 1919, Carroll County, Virginia. He was a Private in the 18th Regiment, Virginia Infantry. He served in Western Virginia, and then merged with the Army of Tennessee. He participated in the campaigns of the army from Chickamauga to Atlanta, moved with Hood to Tennessee and was active in North Carolina. April 9, 1865 his unit merged into the 54th Battalion Virginia Infantry Children:

(1) Abel Surratt, Born 1844, Virginia

(2) Uriah Surratt, Born 1855

(3) Cynthia Surratt, Born 1855, Virginia

(4) McNealey Surratt, Born 1859

(5) Allis Ann Surratt, Born 1863

Generation VII- Isham Surratt, Born August 9, 1811, Grayson County, Virginia; Died June 9, 1883, Carroll County, Virginia; Married: Elizabeth Stantliff, Born January 10,1815, Died January 21, 1900 Children:

(1) James Alfred Surratt, 1832;

(2) Dau St. Surratt, 1830

(3) Savanah Surratt; 1834

(4) Marlinda Surratt, 1887

(5) William I. Surratt, 1850

(6) Patrick Surratt;

(7) Emily A. Surratt, Born 1847

(8) William Patrick Surratt

(9) Elizabeth Surratt, Born 1853

(10) Ribecca Surratt

(11) Atantrila Surratt, Born 1862

Generation VIII- Willis Surratt, Born 1786, Person County, NC, Died 1850 Wythe County, Virginia; Married: Sally, Born 1790, Wythe County, Virginia, Died 1855, Wythe County, Virginia. Children:

(1) Elizabeth Surratt, Born 1807

(2) Cynthia Surratt, Born 1807

(3) Mary P. Surratt, Born 1810

(4) Isham Surratt, Born 1833, Private in Confederate Infantry 29th Regiment, Virginia Infantry. They saw action at Middle Creek, Kentucky, and later saw action in Western Virginia and for a time served in North Carolina under General French. Later he participated in Longstreet Suffolk Expedition and during the Gettysburg Campaign was on detached duty in Tennessee and North Carolina. In the spring of 1864 he returned to Virginia and took place in the Petersburg trenches north and south of the James River and ended the War at Appomattox.

(5) Wiley Surratt, Born 1812

Generation IX- Joseph Surratt, Born 1732, Maryland; Died 1801, NC; Married: Mary, Born 1733, Maryland, Died 1754, North Carolina. Children:

(1) Samuel Surratt, Born 1708

(2) John Surratt, Born 1760

(3) Sebrania Surratt, Born 1766

(4) Unity Surratt, Born 1768

(5) Anna Surratt, Born 1775

(6) Elisha Surratt, Born 1779

(7) Mary Polly Surratt, Born 1789

(8) Willis Surratt, Born 1786

Generation X- Samuel Surratt, Born 1708, Prince George Maryland; Died 1775, Rowan County, NC. Married Anna, (last name unknown) 1st Wife, Born 1708, Died 1749, NC; Married Honour (last name unknown) 2nd Wife; Children:

(1) Samuel Surratt, Born 1738

(2) Rebecca Surratt, Born 1730

(3) Joseph Surratt, Born 1732

(4) Abraham Surratt, Born 1737

(5) Richard Surratt, Born 1743

(6) John Surratt, Born 1760

(7) Thomas Surratt, Born 1750, NC

(8) Allen Surratt, Born 1740, Maryland.

Generation XI- Joseph Surratt, Born 1665, France; Died 1715, Prince Georges, Maryland; Joseph and wife Katherine were among the first families of Prnce Georges County in Maryland. It is believed that he stepped off one of the ships on the Patuxet or Choptank Rivers at the age of 17. Joseph died at the age of 40. Married: Katherine, Born 1667, Prince Georges, Maryland; Died 1717, Prince Georges, Maryland. Court Records show that Katherine was ordered by the courts to present an inventory of their belonging in order to pay her husband's debts. No land was listed, however, she did list the following: "515 pounds of tobacco, 3 Barrels of Indian Corn, 1 Heifer, 1 Calf, 1 old Horse, 1 Mare and Colt, Some old Puter, 1 Churn, some Barrels, 1 Grindstone, 1 Spinning Wheel, Some working tools, 1 Old Trunk, 2 Chests, 1 Bed, 1 Table, and 4 Chairs.." About one year later Katherine presented an amended list under the name Katherine Lewis. These items included One Draft

Horse, 1 Cart, 1 Saddle, Harness, Collar, and one pair of old trunks. Children:

(1) Susana Surratt, Born 1700, St Pauls, Prince Georges, Maryland;

(2) Samuel Surratt, Born 1708, Prince Georges, Maryland;

(3) Joseph Surratt, Born 1710, Mattapany Hundred Area, Prince Georges, Maryland;

Footnotes: Information taken from Mormon Records, Ancestor. com, Carroll County Records, Gilmer Horton, Sandra Llewellyn, Dean Brown, Jeanette Brown Martin,. Roots web.com, Maxine Grove, Wikepedia Encyclopedia, Winston Salem Journal, Watauga Democrat, Wytheville News; Family Bibles, Obituary records of Moody Funeral Home, Clara Chavier and James Horton, U. S. Census Records, and US Social Security Death Index.

Surratt Family Photographs

Annie Myrtle Surratt Horton

Elizabeth Surratt

Sisters, Elizabeth and Annie

Surratt Brother

Unknown Surratt

Surratt Brother

Guy Surratt

Fitzgerald Coat of Arms by Gilmer Horton

Genealogy of Our Fitzgerald Family

(Starting with the most recent generation and counting back)

Generation I- Dean Wayne Brown, Born 1938, Married Eleanor Bradley, Born 1937. (For more detail see Horton Genealogy) Children:

(1) Mark Thomas Brown, Born 1969; Married: Shasta Bode, Date of Marriage 1992; Children: (a) Katherine Elizabeth Brown, Born 1994; (b) John-Henry Samuel Brown, Born 1997 (See Horton Genealogy for details)

(2) Molly Elizabeth Brown, Born 1969: Married 1st Robert Griffin, 1994, Children: Dominick Griffin, Born 2002; 2nd Marriage to Robert Robinson, March 31, 2007. (See Horton Genealogy for details)

Generation II- Katherine Florence Horton, Born June 20, 1920, Wythe, County, Virginia, Died October 5, 2004. Married: Thomas Franklin Brown, Born 1919, Surry County, North Carolina, Died October 1999, Children:

(1) Dean Wayne Brown, Born 1938 (See Generation I)

(2) Roy Leon Brown, Born June 7, 1942; Married Janice Elaine Matthews, Born March 24, 1950; Married June 5, 1965: Children:

(a) Karen Elaine Brown, Born December 5, 1967; Married 1st Keith Helton; 2nd Married John Barber Children:

(1) Brittany Page Helton, Born March 20, 1984;

(2) Brandy Nicolette Helton, Born November 6, 1990

(b) Janice Susan Brown, Born December 5, 1969; Married: 1st Ronald Davis, 2nd Jeffery Bryson, 3rd David Charles Utter Children:

(1) Julia Davis,

(2) Megan Davis

(3) Living Son

(c) Phillip Roy Brown

(d) David Matthew Brown, Born December 5, 1973; Married July 9, 1971 to Jackie Lloyd, Born January 1, 1972; Children:

(1) Carisia Daniell Brown, Born September 24, 2000;

(2) Coby Matthew Brown, Born November 23, 2003

(e) Michael Leon Brown, Born September 1, 1975; Married Lorraine Brown, Born November 23, 2003; Children:

(1) Christian Michael Brown, Born May 13, 2000;

(2) Caitlin Lorraine Brown, Born January 7, 2004

(f) Timothy Gabriel Brown, Born March 25, 1982

(3) Jeanette Brown Martin, Born June 16, 1945; Married 1st, Otis Chappell, Jr. Born March 20, 1943, Died February 13, 2003; Children:

(a) Stephanie Kathleen Chappell, Born November 21, 1970 Married David Warren McDuffie, Born February 15, 1968; Marriage September 13, 1997; Children:

   (1) Kathleen Claire (Katie) McDuffie, Born February 27, 2002;

   (2) Reece Tillman McDuffie, Born August 12, 2003

(b) Julie Anna Chappell, Born August 17, 1973; Married James Stanley Marion, Born February, 13, 1968; Marriage June 5, 1998; Children:

   (1) Anna Elizabeth Marion, Born September 30, 1999;

   (2) Meredith Craig Marion, Born January 9, 2002;

   (3) James Stanley Marion, Jr., Born December 7, 2004; 2nd Marriage Clinton Franklin Martin, May 6, 2007

Generation III- Marvin Chester Horton, Born, January 24, 1897; Died January 24, 1964. Forsyth County, NC. Married Annie Myrtle Surratt, Born 1897; Died February 25, 1982. Children:

(a) Gilmer, Born 1916;

(b) Ruth, Born 1918;

(c) Katherine, Born 1920;

(d) Helen, Born 1922;

(e) Mazie, Born 1924, Died 2006;

(f) Daniel, Born 1927;

(g) Jean, Born 1932 (See Horton Genealogy for more details)

Generation IV- Mickie Ann Fitzgerald, Born Carroll County, Virginia; Died Carroll County, Virginia. Married James Surratt, Born 1877,

Virginia, Died, Virginia. Children: Annie, 1897; Joseph, Martha, Samuel, Elizabeth and Guy; Children:

(1) Elizabeth Surratt

(2) Annie Surratt

(3) Arthur Surratt

(4) Guy Surratt

(5) Joseph Surratt

Generation V- James (or William) Fitzgerald, Born Virginia; Married Martha Cave, Born 1885, Virginia; Children:

(1) William Fitzgerald, Born 1806; Died 1925; Children: (had 7 children);

(2) Mickie Ann Fitzgerald, Born Carroll County, James fought in the Civil War and was killed in action. Martha married Mr. James McHone; they had 2 children (names not known)

Generation VI- Robert Fitzgerald 1795, Probably Born in Ireland; Lived at Regent Street, Lambeth. Later he is an accountant living at Marlborough Street, Southwark, and later at Jane Street in 1839 a settlement examination at St. Mary Newington showed he and his family had lived at 5 Temple Street about 1832. On the 1851 census states he is at 6 Staple Buildings, Holborm with his wife and three children, and is out of business. He was present at the death of his son Robert Francis Fitzgerald.

Married Susanna Redmonds, Born 1797, Ireland; At her marriage she signed her name as being especially associated with Dublin, Wexford and Wicklow. Children:

(1) Mary Ann Fitzgerald, Born 1814

(2) Samuel Fitzgerald, Born 1816

(3) Robert Francis Fitzgerald, Born 1823; Married Julia, Born 1824. She was born in Ireland. Her children were born in Southwark and Holborn. At the time of the 1851 census the family was living in Blackfriars. She appears to have survived her husband. Children:

(a) Robert Francis Richard Fitzgerald, Born 1846;

(b) Catherine Fitzgerald, Born 1848 in Holborn and Baptized on December 9th, 1851 at St. Andrews, Holborn, London, with her brother and sister, Just after her father's death, living at 21 Baldwin Gardens. At her marriages she signed X, In 1866 she was living at 4b James Street, Walworth. She appears on the 1881 census at 124 Penton Place, Walworth, Care of St. Marks Church as head of the household but not yet a widow. She died around 1899. Married James Bacon, Marriage Date 1856, St Mary, Lambeth, London. On his marriage certificate he signed his name and was a bachelor, of official age, a hawker, living at King Street. His father was Samuel bacon, a carpenter. James was alive at the time of the 1881 census but must have died soon after wards. Married John Matthews, Born 1856-1930; Lived at 39 Trafalgar Street, Walworth; On his marriage certificate he was a fireman at a foundry, a bachelor aged 29, living at 10 Beddome Street, Walworth and he signed X on Lydia's birth certificate he is an Iron Founders Furnace Man. After his wife's death, he lived with his son John. He probably died at St. Thomas's Hospital, London about 1930; Children of Catherine and James:

(a) Henry, Born 1866;

(b) Catherine, Born 1871;

(c) James, Born 1873; Caroline, Born 1875;

Children of Catherine and John:

(d) Susanna Fitzgerald, Born 1825

(e) Amelia Fitzgerald, Born 1826

(f) Edward Fitzgerald, Born 1633

(g) Juliet Fitzgerald, Born 1830

(h) Charles Fitzgerald, Born 1833

(i) Jessie Fitzgerald, Born 1833

(j) Theresa Fitzgerald, Born 1841

Footnotes: Information taken from Mormon Records, Ancestor. com, Carroll County Records, Gilmer Horton, Sandra Llewellyn, Dean Brown, Jeanette Brown Martin,. Roots web.com, Maxine Grove, Wikepedia Encyclopedia, Winston Salem Journal, Watauga Democrat, Wytheville News; Family Bibles, Obituary records of Moody Funeral Home, Clara Chavier and James Horton, U. S. Census Records, and US Social Security Death Index.

History of the Cave Family

My grandmother, Annie Myrtle Surratt's mother was Mickie Fitzgerald. Mickie's father, James Fitzgerald, married Martha Cave. Martha was born in 1885. The Cave family is an interesting family of ancestors to follow. I have been able to trace this line twenty-four generations.

The Cave surname dates back hundreds of years in Europe. Many researchers feel it is Scottish-Irish in origin. On the other hand, other researchers feel it is French or German Huguenots. The first notable Cave was Wymarus deCave, who came to Yorkshire, England with "William the Red" in 1069. The Cave families began to appear in America about the year, 1720. Benjamin Cave, one of our relatives, was the first Cave family who came to America. Records reveal that Benjamin settled in Orange County, Virginia, between 1630 and 1700. Benjamin and his family remained loyal to the Church of England in Virginia until several of the Cave family members became pioneers and changed to Baptist and Methodist in the new world of the Virginia frontier.

About 1734 a large area in Virginia which had been called St. Mark and St George Parishes were reorganized into what is now called Orange and Spotsylvania Counties.

Some early documents of 1736 show a partition in Orange County Virginia Court for judgment against Joseph Cave for a debt of 1,000 pounds of tobacco. This was his taxes, for at this time farmers were paying taxes in pounds of tobacco, since money was almost nonexistent. He could not be located and the charges were dismissed in Court in 1736. On September 1742 the Orange county Court ordered the churchwarden of St.Mark's Parrish to bind out the children of Joseph Cave because "He takes no care for their education nor cause them to be brought up in Christian Principles".

One of his sons, William Cave was already apprenticed out to someone else. Anyway, Joseph left the village and crossed the mountains and became a pioneer into what is now Page County, Virginia. The case was dismissed in May 1748.

Civil War Relatives from the Cave Family

Benjamin Cave G (7) Grandfather (XI-4) 1710-1762, served as a Lieutenant to Captain John Scott in the Virginia Colonial Militia.

My G (6) Grandfather, John Cave (IX) of 1758 served in the 2nd Virginia Regiment until 1777. His sons Benjamin Cave, Ruben Cave, William Cave, and John all served in the Revolutionary War conflict. They would have been 7th cousins.

G (7) Grandfather, Benjamin Cave (VIII) of 1787 was a pioneer and fought in the Indian Wars in the Ohio Valley, He also fought in the Revolutionary War as a soldier.

G (3) Uncle, Benjamin F Cave (VII- 6) of 1849, He fought as a Private for the Confederate Calvary, 2nd Virginia Regiment.

G (3) Grandfather, Private Calvin H. Cave served in the Confederate Infantry, 35th Virginia Regiment.

G (2) Uncle, Private, Calvin H. Cave, He served in the Confederate Infantry, 33rd Virginia Regiment. (Died of pneumonia)

G (2) Uncle, Private John Cave, He served in the Confederate Artillery, Donald's Co., Virginia Light Infantry.

G (2) Uncle, Private Return Cave, He served in the 97th Regiment, Virginia Militia, Spitler's Regiment.

G. (2) Uncle, Private Samuel L. Cave, He served in the 97th Regiment, Virginia Militia.

G (2) Uncle, Private W. A. Cave, 3rd Regiment, Virginia Infantry, Local Defense (Henley's and Mc Amermey's Infantry

Cousin (6) Private, Paschal Washington Cave (1839) 12th Company H. Virginia Infantry 33, CSA. – Shoemaker and minister

Cave Family Crest
By Gilmer F. Horton

Our Cave Family Genealogy

(Starting with the most recent generations and counting back)

Generation I- Dean Wayne Brown, Born 1938, Married Eleanor Bradley, Born 1937. Children:

(1) Mark Thomas Brown;

(2) Molly Elizabeth Brown (See Horton Genealogy for details)

Generation II- Katherine Florence Horton, Born 1920, Wythe, County, Virginia; Died October 5, 2004; Married Thomas Franklin Brown, Born 1919, Surry County, North Carolina. Died October 1999; Children:

(1) Dean Wayne Brown;

(2) Roy Leon Brown;

(3) Jeanette Brown (See Horton Genealogy for details)

Generation III- Annie Myrtle Surratt, Born 1897, Carroll County Virginia, Died February 25, 1982, Surry County, NC; Married Marvin Chester Horton, Born January 24, 1897, Virginia; Died February 24, 1964, Forsyth County, NC. Children:

(1) Gilmer, 1916;

(2) Ruth, 1918;

(3) Katherine, 1920;

(4) Helen; 1922,

(5) Mazie 1924;

(6) Daniel, 1927;

(7) Jean, 1932 (See Horton Genealogy for details)

Generation IV- Mickie Fitzgerald Born Carroll County, Virginia; Died Carroll County, Virginia; Married to James Surratt, Born 1877, Virginia; Died Virginia; Children:

(1) Annie, Born 1897,

(2) Joseph,

(3) Martha,

(4) Samuel,

(5) Elizabeth,

(6) Guy

Generation V- Martha Cave, Born 1885, Virginia, Died Virginia. Married to James Fitzgerald, Born Virginia; Children: Had 7 children

Generation VI- Calvin H. Cave, Born 1840, Virginia, Died 1922, Virginia. Served in the Civil War as a Confederate Soldier, Private in Infantry, 35th Regiment of Virginia. Married: Julia Ann Lucas, Born, 1843, Virginia; Died 1908, Virginia. Children:

(1) Elizabeth,

(2) Bessie,

(3) George,

(4) Charles,

(5) Mary,

(6) Annie,

(7) John,

(8) Isaac,

(9) Bettie,

(10) Daisy,

(11) Birdie,

(12) Frank,

(13) Martha,

(14) Manuel,

(15) Maude,

(16) Fred Born 1887

Generation VII- John A. Cave, Born 1812, Virginia; Died 1899, Virginia. John Served as a Private in the Confederate Artillery, Donald's Company, Virginia Light Infantry. He was a preacher and blacksmith in the 1850 Census. He lived in the Marksville District of Page County, Virginia. Married: Mary Ann Phillips, Born 1818, Virginia; Died 1899, Virginia. Children:

(1) Samuel. Born 1837, Served as a Private in 97th Reg., Virginia Militia;

(2) Calvin Born 1840, served as a Private in 97th Reg., Va. Militia, (Spitler's);

(3) Eliza Born 1844;

(4) Mary Born 1846;

(5) Benjamin Born 1849, Served as a Private in Confederate Calvary, 2nd Regiment of Virginia;

(6) John, 1850, served as a Private in the Confederate Artillery, Donald's Co., Virginia Light Inf.

Generation VIII- Benjamin Cave, Born 1787, Virginia, Died Virginia; He Served as Private in the Confederate Calvary, 2nd Regiment. Benjamin became a minister of the Gospel serving in Carolinas, Virginia, Kentucky and Ohio. Married: Nance Gillihue, Born 1818, Virginia, Died 1899, Virginia. Children:

(1) Harriett Cave, Born 1808, Married to Aaron Offenbaker; George, 1809

(2) Elizabeth Cave, Born, 1810

(3) Paschal Wellington Cave, Born 1810 and Died 1896. Paschal was a shoemaker and had 8 children and was married to Elizabeth Offenbacker. He had a son named Washington who served in the Civil War Company H, 33rd Inf, and was an army shoemaker. He is listed as a member of the Episcopal Church. Washington is buried at Pine Grove, Page County, Virginia, 1917

(4) Edward Cave, Born 1911

(5) Katherine Cave, Born 1812

(6) John Cave, Born 1812

(7) Joseph Cave, Born 1817

(8) Benjamin Cave, Born 1819; Benjamin served in the Revolutionary War. Records show that in the early 1800's Benjamin Cave lived in Fox Hollow, on one of the upper branches of the Hawksbill Creek, just beyond the community of Marksville against the Blue Ridge Mountains, some few miles beyond the little town of Stanley, in what is now Page County. Benjamin of Hawksville married Nancy of Rapid Ann River, probably from Culpeper. Her real name was Nancy Gallihue. Benjamin and Nancy had 11 children. Benjamin's wife was Dicy Runkle, they were married in 1839. Both were members of the Myrtle Tree Church, where Dicy's brother was preacher.

Later they moved to Indiana where they purchased 60 acres of land in the Jackson Township on the Eel River bend. Benjamin was also involved in the bloody battles of the Indians vs. the settlers and took to the bottle in his later years and was recorded by local officials for beating his wife.

One Son of Benjamin and Dicy was Perry, who was married to Sarah Elizabeth Baumgadtner. They lived in the southeast corner of the County next to Whitley County, Indiana. Perry owned 40 acres of land and he planted a big garden every year. They had their own eggs, cheese, milk and meats. They sold butter and milk if they could spare it. They planted sorghum cane and in the fall made molasses and sold most of it to neighbors. They raised fruit in their orchards and made cider. They had homemade wine and kept bees for their honey. Neighbors would take the older children to work on their farms and homes for room, board and new clothes and shoes for fall school. Perry died of gangrene of the feet, caused by Diabetes.

(9) William Cave, Born 1820, Served in the Revolutionary War. William Arrell returned to Page County, Virginia and married Mary Ann Roads in 1848. He died in 1888 and is buried in the

Lutheran cemetery at Woodstock, Virginia. William became a lawyer in 1850.

(10)   Sarah Cave, Born 1827

(11)   Mary Dorcas Cave, Born 1817

Generation IX- John Cave, Born 1758, Virginia; Died 1825, Virginia. He served in the 2nd Virginia Regiment from October through December of 1777 and was regularly discharged. He was drafted again 1780, but since he was recently married, he sent his brother Benjamin Cave, who volunteered to take his place. Married: Catherine, Born 1758; Children:

(1) Lucy Cave, Born 1772

(2) Jonas Cave, Born 1774

(3) Thomas Cave, Born 1775

(4) Sally Cave, Born 1776

(5) Joseph Cave, Born 1777

(6) Noah Cave, Born 1778

(7) Rubin Cave, Born 1781

(8) William Cave, Born 1782

(9) Rhonda Cave, Born 1784

(10) Molly Cave, Born 1785

(11) Nancy Cave, Born 1789

(12) John Cave, Born 1790

(13) Sarah Cave, Born 1794

(14) Elizabeth Cave, Born 1809

(15) Noah Cave, Born 1844

(16) Benjamin Cave, Born 1787; Records show that all the children were born in Madison County, Virginia.

Generation X- Joseph Cave, Born 1758, Died 1862 (104) Champaign County, Ohio; Married: Mary Jenkins; Children:

(1) Ruben Cave, Born 1738

(2) William Cave, Born 1749

(3) John Cave, Born 1758

(4) Benjamin Cave, Born 1760

(5) Thomas Cave, Born 1775

(6) Ruben Cave, Born 1880

Generation XI- David Cave, Born 1690, Virginia; Died 1756, Virginia. Married: Sarah Moore; Children:

(1) John Born 1710;

(2) David;

(3) James;

(4) Benjamin Born 1703 in Windsor County, Berkshire, England, He Died 1762 at Montebello, Culpeper, Virginia. Benjamin was married to Hannah Bledsoe 1727, in Spotsylvania County. Benjamin was among the members of the first vestry of St. Mark's in 1731 (St. Mark's Parish, Culpeper, Virginia) He was vestryman. He lived for a time at what is now known as Rhodes in Orange, and then moved to land on the Upper Rapidan River near Cave's Ford, which derives its name from him. Benjamin was a Lieutenant to Captain John Scott in the Virginia Colonial Militia. He was Sheriff of Orange County, Virginia. Children:

   (1) Sarah;

(2) Joseph Born 1758, Virginia

Generation XII- John Cave, Born 1637, England; Died 1721, Stafford England; Wife: Elizabeth Travers, Born 1650, Caldecott, England; Children:

(1) Sarah Cave, Born 1670, England

(2) David Cave, Born 1690, Virginia;

(3) John Cave

Generation XIII- Samuel Cave, Born 1599, Great Leighs Essex, England; Died 1666, Braintree, England. Married: Rachel Kellogg, Born 1600, Great Leights, England, Died 1665, Brantree, England; Children:

(1) Nathaniel Cave, Born 1630, England

(2) Rachael Cave Born in England

(3) Phoebe Cave, Born 1626, England

(4) Mary Cave, Born 1628, England

(5) John Cave, Born 1637, England

(6) Richard Cave

Generation XIV- John Cave was Born 1550, England. Wife unknown, Children:

(1) Samuel Cave, Born 1599, Essex, England

Generation (not known)- Wymarus deCave, Born 1009, English Title: "The Lordship of Manor deCave, Lord of North and South Cave, Cliffe, Stanton, Newland, Skalyyer, and Manor of Waldingstone in County of Ebor." Migrated from France or Germany; He came into North

Yorkshier, England with 'William the Red' and was given a manor in Yorkshire.

Footnotes: Information taken from Mormon Records, Ancestor. com, Carroll County Records, Gilmer Horton, Sandra Llewellyn, Dean Brown, Jeanette Brown Martin,. Roots web.com, Maxine Grove, Wikepedia Encyclopedia, Winston Salem Journal, Watauga Democrat, Wytheville News; Family Bibles, Obituary records of Moody Funeral Home, Clara Chavier and James Horton, U. S. Census Records, and US Social Security Death Index.

Interesting Documents of
the Horton Families

The following pages are copies of the notes from Gilmer Horton's files on the family Crest. He spent many years while serving in Europe researching the Horton Family Crest.

Sketch # 1 by Gilmer F. Horton

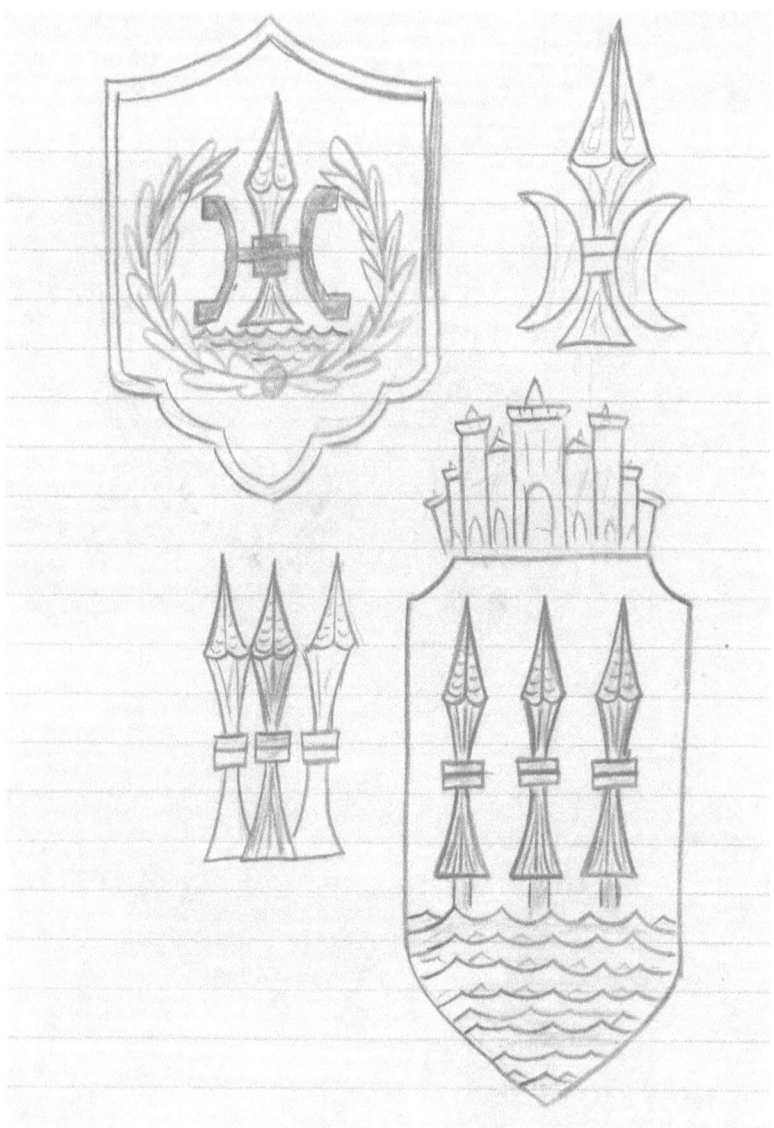

Sketch # 2, by Gilmer F. Horton

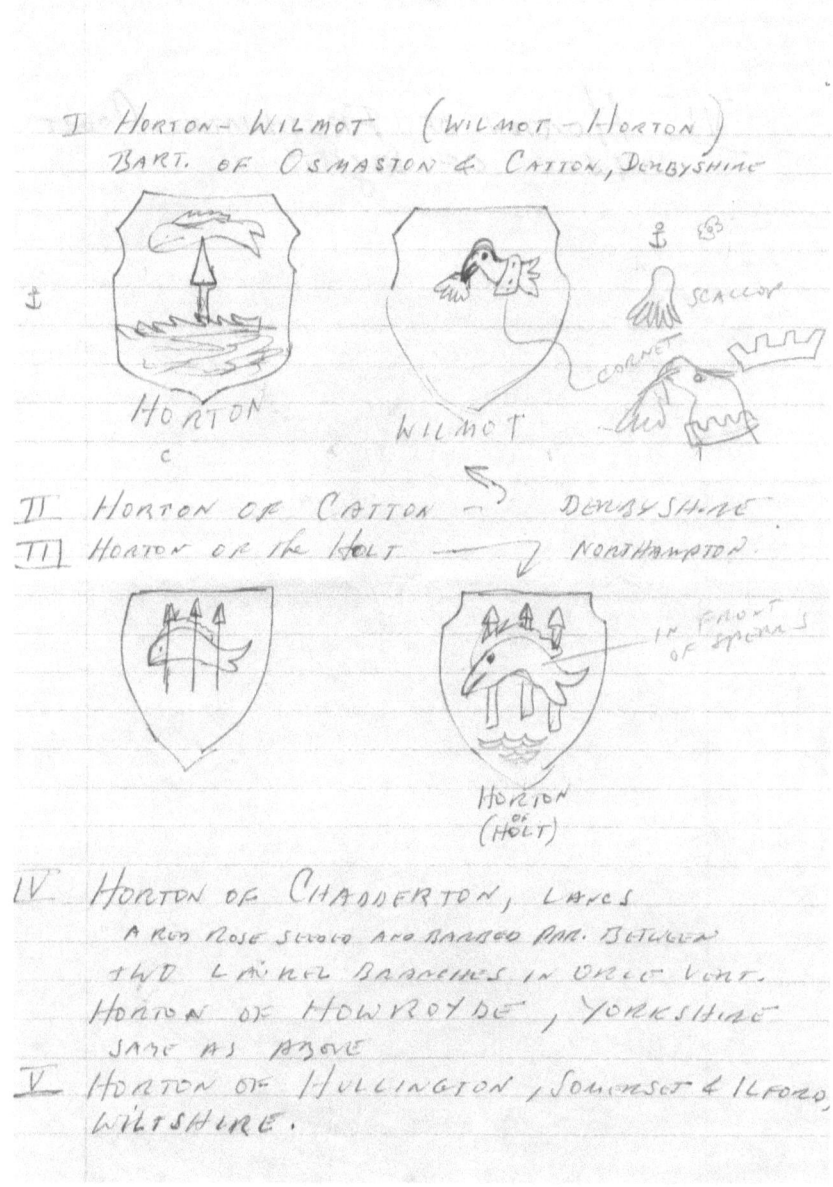

I. Horton - Wilmot (Wilmot - Horton)
Bart. of Osmaston & Catton, Derbyshire

HORTON

WILMOT

SCALLOP

CORNET

II. Horton of Catton — Derbyshire
III. Horton of the Holt — Northampton.

IN FRONT OF SPEARS

HORTON OF (HOLT)

IV. Horton of Chadderton, Lancs
A Red Rose Slipped and Barbed Ppr. Between
Two Laurel Branches in Orle Vert.
Horton of Howroyde, Yorkshire
Same as above

V. Horton of Hullington, Somerset & Ilford,
Wiltshire.

Sketch # 3, by Gilmer F. Horton

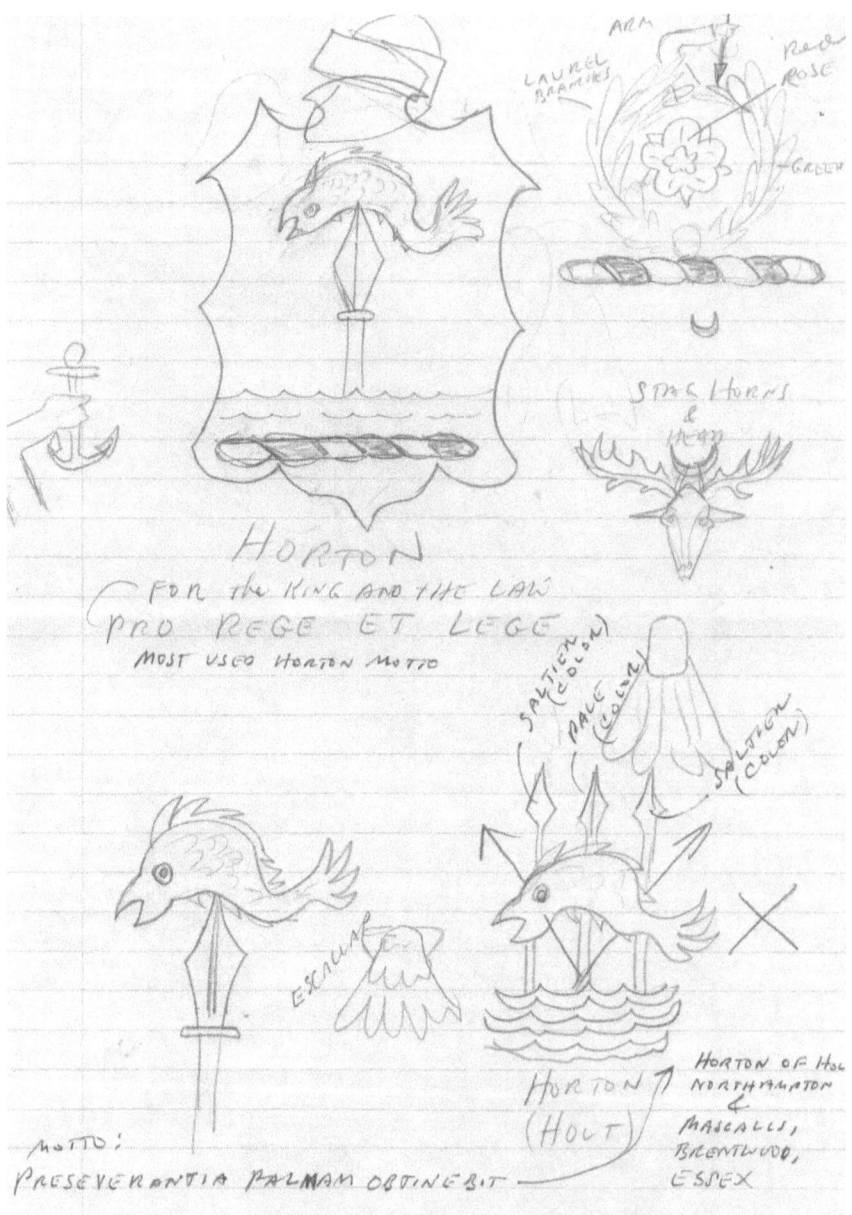

Sketch # 4, by Gilmer F. Horton

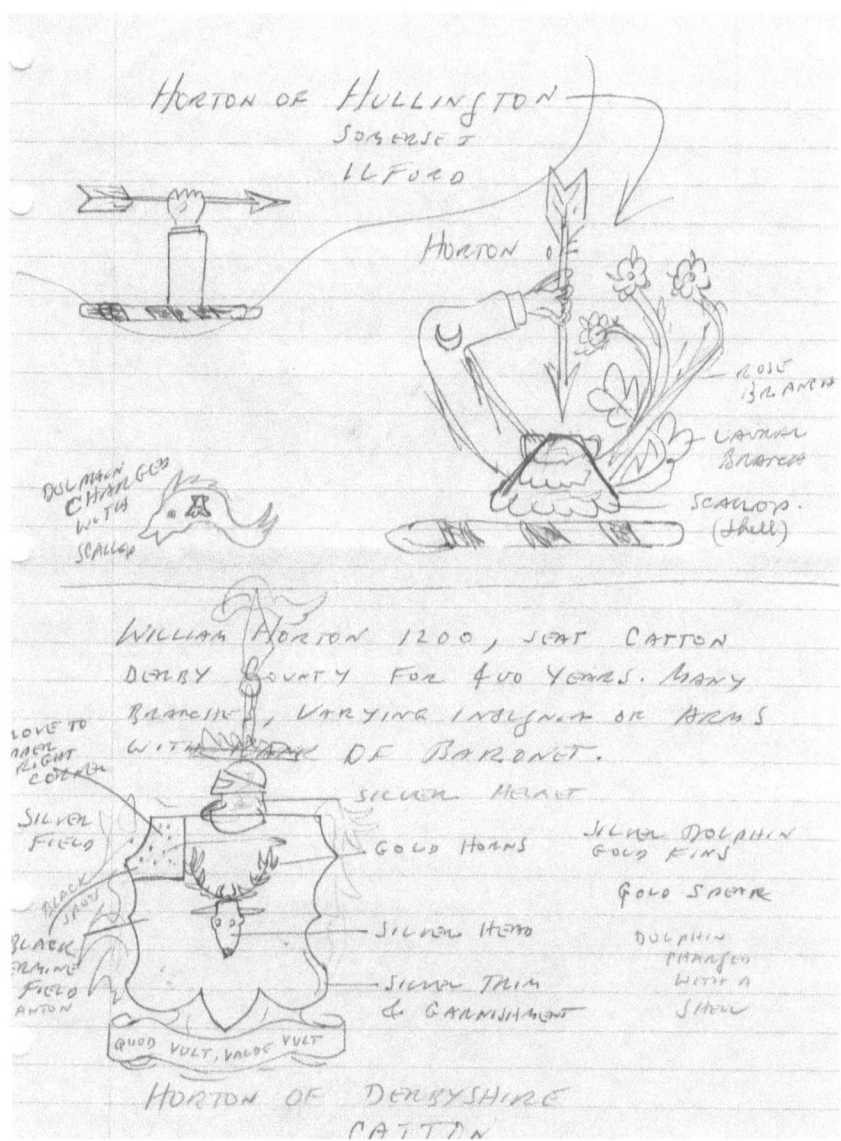

Sketch # 5, by Gilmer F. Horton

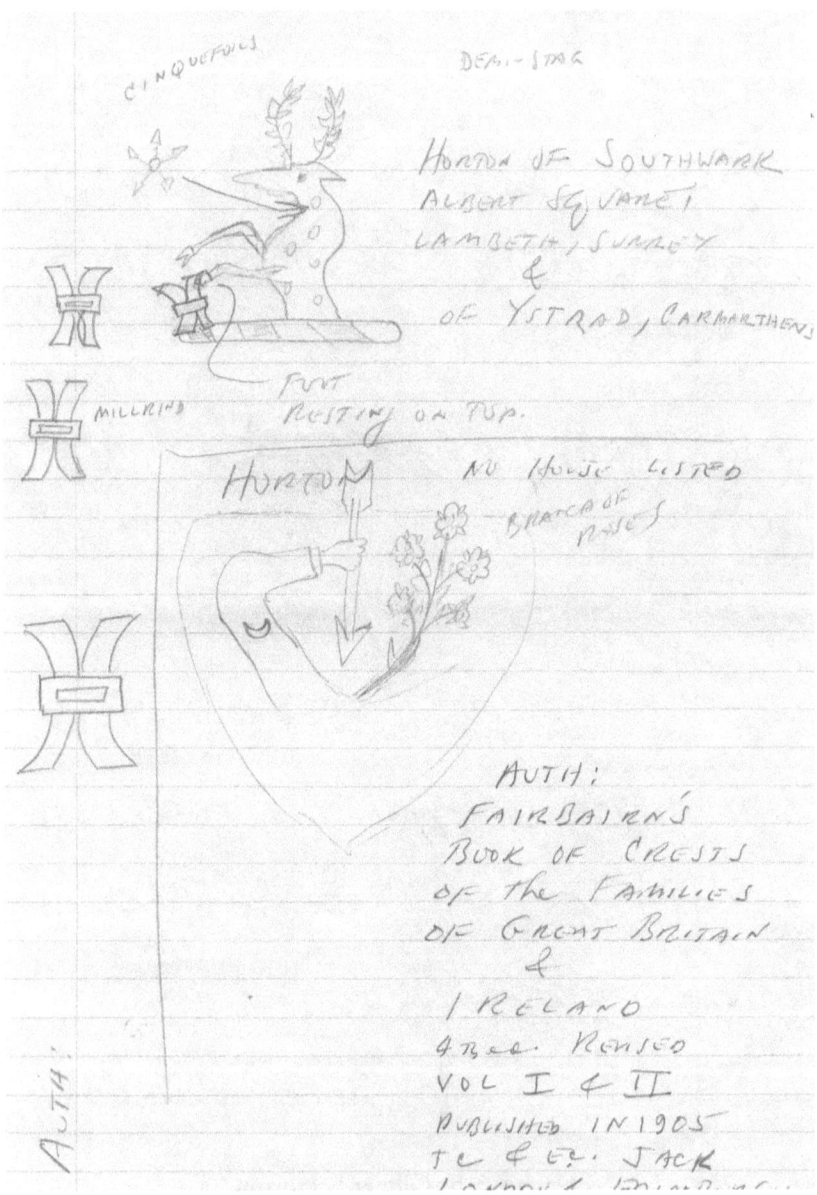

Sketch #6, by Gilmer F. Horton

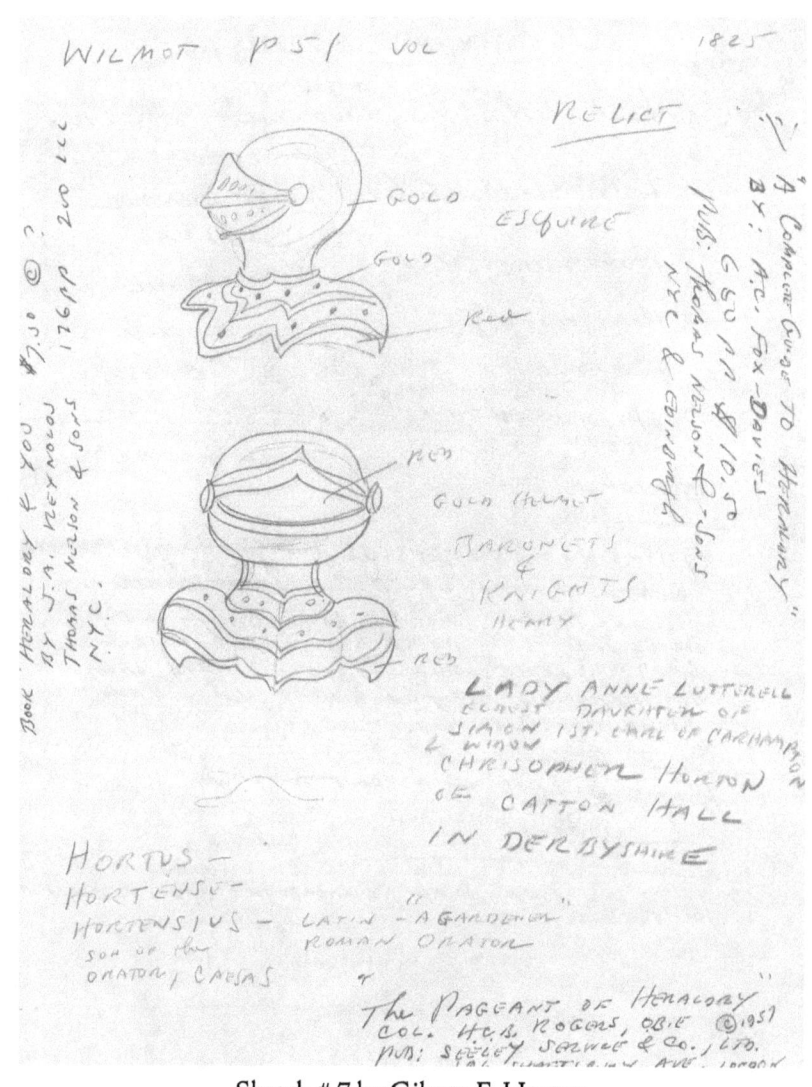

Sketch # 7 by Gilmer F. Horton

UNITED STATES DEPARTMENT OF JUSTICE

FEDERAL BUREAU OF INVESTIGATION

WASHINGTON 25, D. C.

June 8, 1955

T-Sgt. Gilmer F. Horton, AF-34001331
Hq. Sqdn. 98th Bombardment Wing
Lincoln Air Force Base
Lincoln, Nebraska

Dear Mr. Horton:

I have received your letter of May 31, 1955,
making inquiry about the FBI National Academy. Although
the Academy is primarily designed for representatives
of state, county and city law enforcement agencies,
we do, on a limited number of occasions, have repre-
sentatives of other organizations in attendance and
we have had a few men from the armed services. Requests
for the attendance of representatives in the armed
services, however, must be submitted to this Bureau
by the Washington headquarters of the branch of the
service concerned.

I would like to point out, however, that the
curriculum of the National Academy is designed
primarily for training police instructors and police
executives. I trust that the above information will
be of assistance to you.

Sincerely yours,

J. Edgar Hoover

One of two letters to Gilmer Horton from J. Edgar Hoover

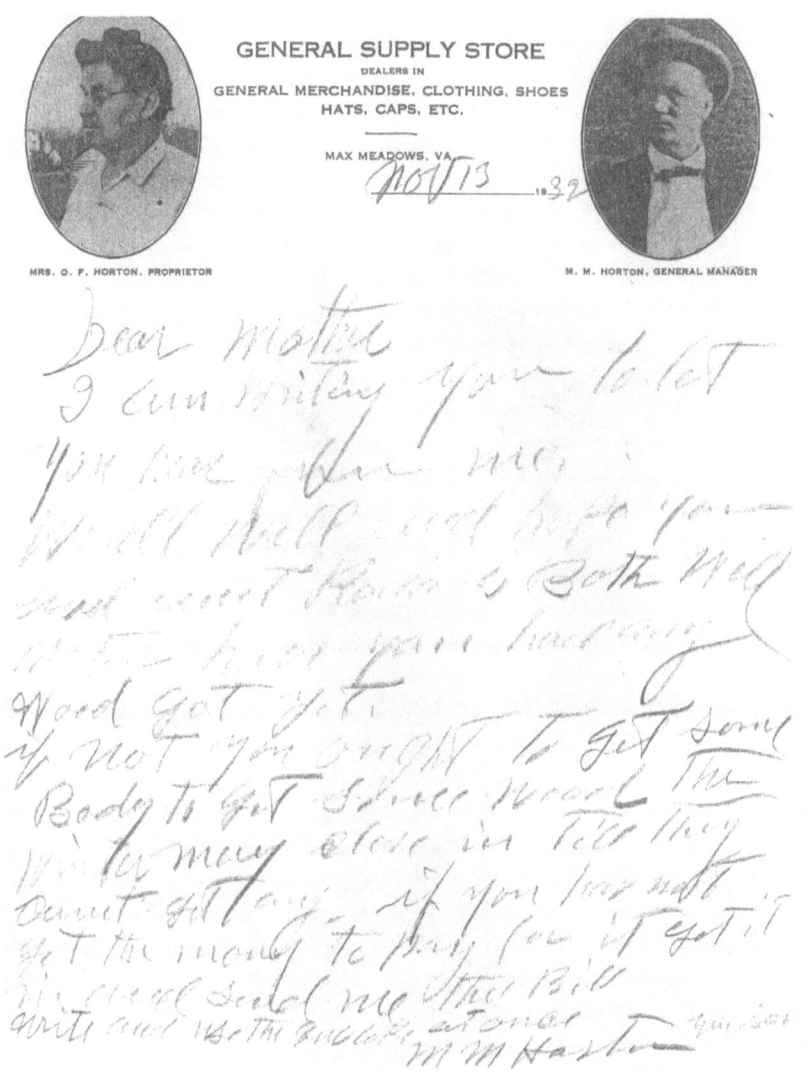

Letter from M. M. Horton to his Mother, Dated 1932

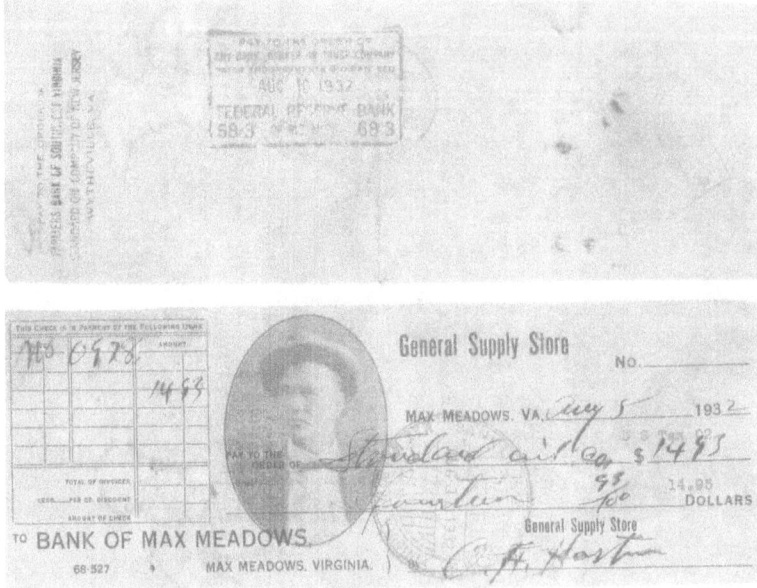

Check from the Horton Store in Max Meadows, VA

1893 Registration Card for John W. Horton

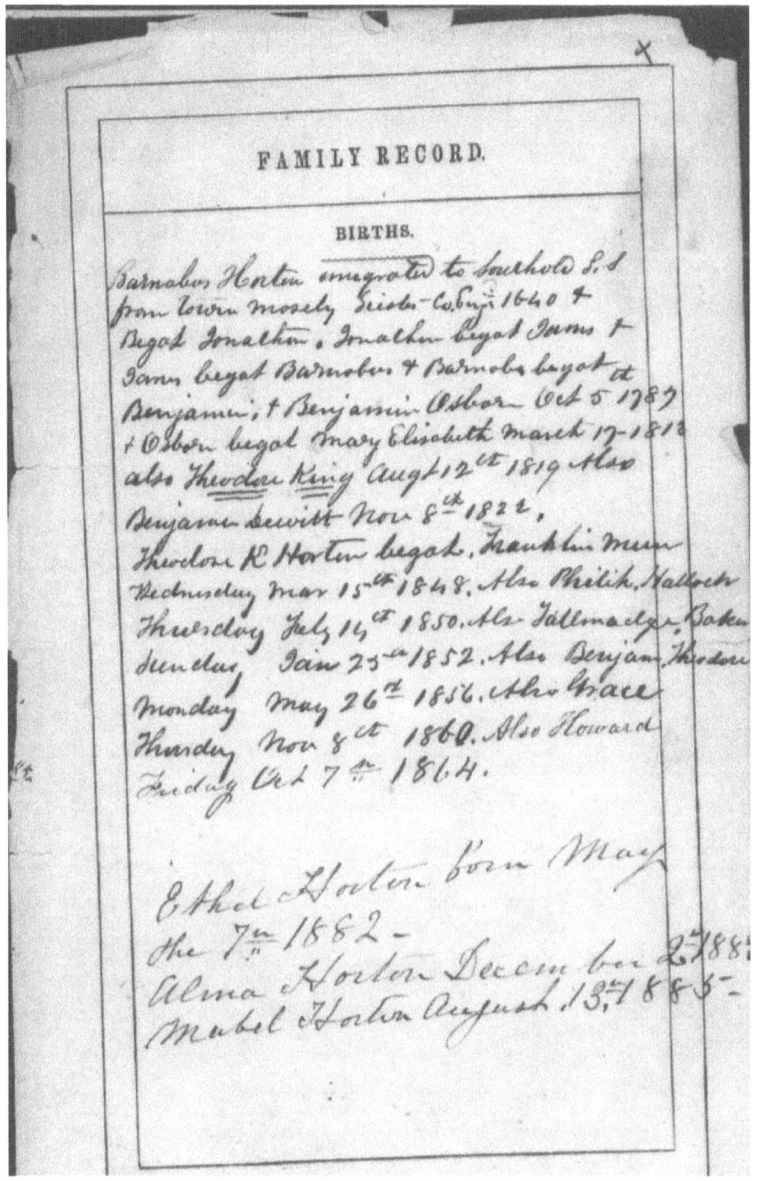

Horton Family Birth Records from 1640

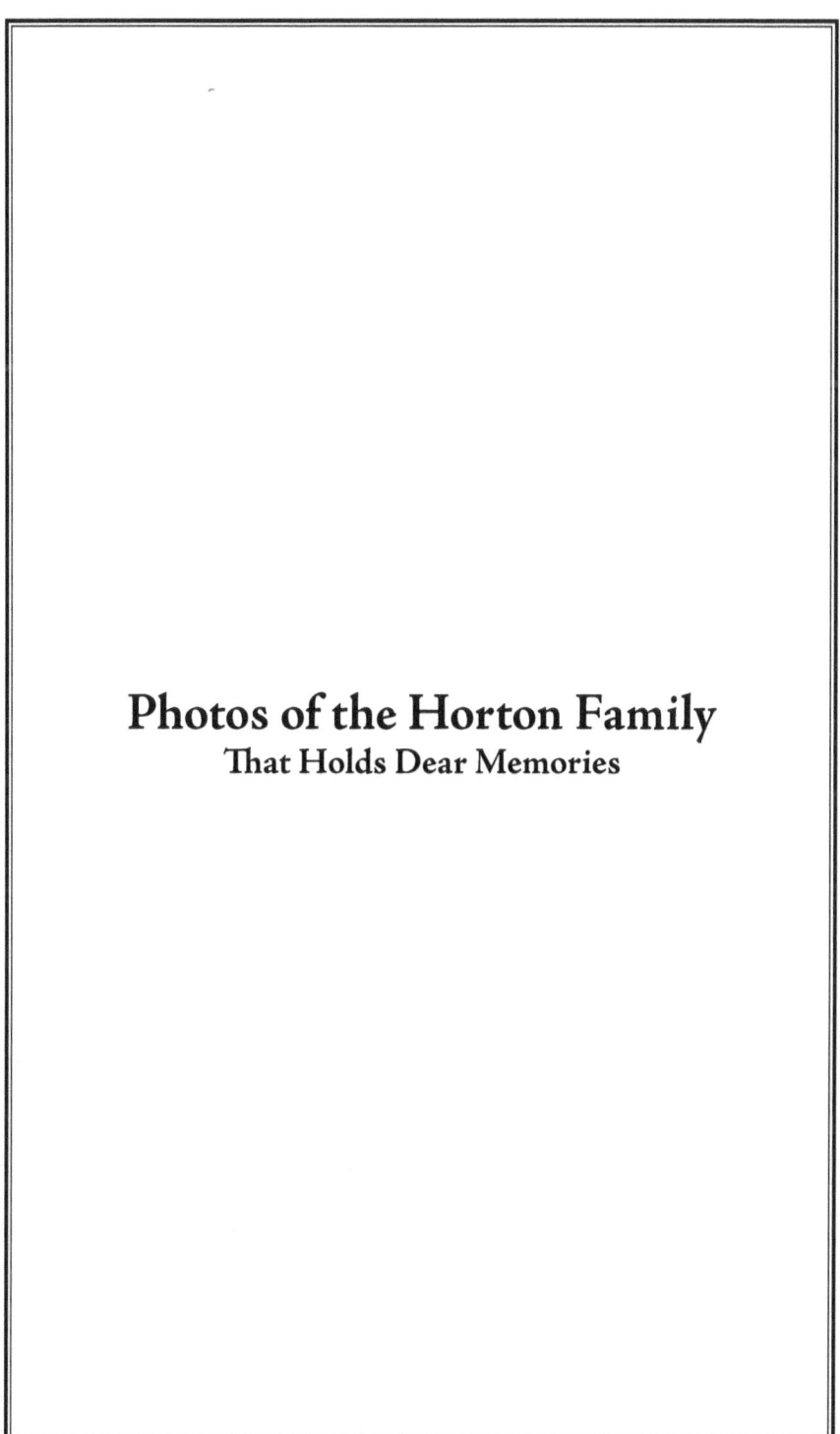

Photos of the Horton Family
That Holds Dear Memories

Gilmer Horton about 1948

Ruth and Buddy Goins in the 1960's

Katherine and Tom Brown with Santa

Helen and Arnold Draughn about 1958

Mazie Dara In Mount Airy 1982

Tommy and Mazie Dara

Jean Horton Gabriel

Gus Gabriel

Aunt Susie Grove, Always a delight

Annie Myrtle Surratt Horton

Grandma Horton at Disneyland, California

Edward Cave about 1935

Dan and Frances Horton Wedding Picture

American Revolutionary Soldiers

Horton, Caleb: Westchester County Militia, First Regiment, Enlisted Man, Buried in the Chester Congregational Church Yard, Morris County, NJ

Horton, Colonel Nathan: Born 1720, Captain Nathan Horton served in the Rev. War after moving to Roxbury, NJ from Southold, Suffolk County, NY. He served as a captain with Coris County, NJ Militia in the Rev. Army from 1777 to 1778 and was said to have been a man of upstanding character. He became known as Colonel Nathan Horton when he served as Colonel of the Regiment of the militia for Ash County, NC

Isaac DeHaven: Born February 16, 1750 in Loudoun County , Virginia. Great (x5) uncle; was a member of Captain Henry Lee's Company of Virginia Cavalry and was involved in several skirmishes near Philadelphia. He was discharged in December 1778. He was a corpal.

Abraham DeHaven: Born 1747, Loudon, Virginia; Great (x6) uncle fought in the Revolutionary War as a Private in for the Pennsylvania Troops.

Peter DeHaven: Born December 3, 1686, Mulheim, Westfalen, Germany; Great (x 8) uncle fought in the Revolutionary War as a Private for the Continental Troops.

Edward DeHaven: Born 1713, Great (x 9) uncle fought in the Revolutionary War as a Private for the Continental Troops.

John DeHaven: Born 1715, Great (x 9) uncle fought in the Revolutionary War as a Private for the Pennsylvania Troops.

DeHaven, Samuel: Born 1746- 1821, fought in the Revolutionary War for the Pennsylvannia Troops. Great (x 9) uncle.

Cave, Benjamin, (XI-4) 1710-1762, served as a Lieutenant to Captain John Scott in the Virginia Colonial Militia.

Cave, John: (G x 6), (Generation IX) of 1758, served in the 2nd Virginia Regiment until 1777.

Cave, Benjamin: (G x 7), (Generation VIII) of 1787 was a pioneer and fought in the Indian Wars in Ohio Valley. He also fought in the Revolutionary War as a soldier.

Snake Creek Homeplace, Photo by Gail Josey

Confederate Ancestors in the Civil War

HORTON. AARON: Co. I. Age 10 in 1850 CCC. Enl. 8/10/61 at Hillsville. He died at Blue Sulphur Springs, 10/31/61.

HORTON, ANDREW: Co. I. Age 21 in 1850 Smyth Co. census. Enl. 8/10/61 at Hillsville. Sick 10/61. Captured at Piedmont, 6/5/64. POW Camp Morton. He died in prison from inflamed lungs, 12/6/64. Bur. Green Lawn Cem., grave #1191.

HORTON, CHARLES: Co. F. PWR.

HORTON, HENDERSON: Co. I. Enl. 8/10/61 at Hillsville. Present 12/61 then NFR. He died in Carroll Co. 9/28/1885, age 50.

HORTON, HENRY, JR.: Co. I. Enl. 8/10/61 at Hillsville. Sick 9/61. He deserted 5/15/62. Present on final roll. He received clothing 4th qtr. 1864. Living in Carroll Co. in 1910, age 77.

HORTON, JACOB: Co. I. Age 9 in 1850 CCC. Enl. 9/15/62 at Zollicoffer. Present on final roll. Living in Carroll Co. in 1880.

HORTON, JOHN RILEY: Co. I. Enl. 8/10/61 at Hillsville. Sick 10/61. He lost a thumb at Fayetteville. Captured at Winchester, 9/19/64. POW Pt. Lookout. Exch. 3/15/65. Living in Carroll Co. in 1900, age 68.

HORTON, JOSEPH: Co. I. Born 2/29/36. Enl. in 1862. He died 12/4/1914, bur. in Independence.

HORTON, VINCENT: Co. I. Age 24 in 1850 CCC. Enl. 8/10/61 at Hillsville. Sick 9/61. Captured at Piedmont, 6/5/64. POW Camp Morton. Exch. 3/4/65. In Rich. Hosp. 3/11/65. He died 2/22/1918.

DEHAVEN, ISSAC W.: Co. I. Age 14 in 1850 CCC. Sick when the regt. moved from Wytheville, 7/12/61. He died at White Sulphur Springs from fever, 11/23/62.

JOSEPH DEHAVEN: 114th Regiment of the Pennsylvania Infantry of the Union Army.

JOHN DEHAVEN: Union Infantry, 51st Regiment, Pennsylvania Infantry, 88th Regiment, Pennsylvania Infantry.

ISAAC DEHAVEN: Born 1838, Private in Virginia Militia, Confederate Army.

FITZGERALD, Charles: born 1833, Virginia; 34th Regiment Virginia Infantry, Private, Company C

FITZGERALD, James: or William, 3rd Regiment, Virginia Calvary, Sergeant when killed. My G, G, Grandfather

CAVE, JOHN A.: Born 1812, Served as a Private in Confederate Artillery, Donald's Company Virginia Light Infantry. He was a preacher and blacksmith.

CAVE, BENJAMIN F: (gx7 grandfather) (generation VII-6) of 1849 fought as a Private in the Confederate Calvary, 2nd Virginia Regiment.

CAVE, CALVIN H: (gx2 uncle) fought as a Private in the Confederate Infantry, 35th Virginia Regiment; he died of pneumonia.

CAVE, RETURN: (gx2 uncle) fought in 97th Regiment, Virginia Militia, Spitler's Regiment.

CAVE, SAMUEL L: (gx2 uncle) fought in the 97th Regiment, Virginia Militia.

CAVE, W.A: (gx2 uncle) fought as a Private in the 3rd Regiment, Virginia Infantry, Local Defense (Henley's and McAmemey's Infantry.

CAVE, PASCHAL WASHINGTON: (Cousin x 6) of 1839, fought in 12th Company H, Virginia Infantry 33, CSA as a Shoemaker and Minister.

Gilmer Horton and Friends
May 14, 1945, Trieste

Jean Horton 13 years old   Jean Horton at 17 years old

Tibitha McMillian, Born September 7, 1854

Ruth Horton Goins and Bud Goins

Grandma Horton's Church Dress, Hat and Apron
(Photo by Eleanor Brown)

About the Author

Dean Brown has spent many years being involved in historical projects in and around Mount Airy, North Carolina. He is a past member of the Surry County Historical Society, past member of the Horne Creek Historical Farm, past member of the Mount Airy Historical Commission and an elected City Commissioner. He has collected oral histories of the Blue Ridge Mountains for the past 25 years and uses much of his material in his writings. Brown was instrumental in getting the Mount Airy Sons of Confederate Veterans Camp started and was the camp adjutant for many years. He was the NC State Adjutant for the Sons of Confederate Veterans for 4 years. He grew up a few miles from the original birthplace of James Ewell Brown Stuart (Gen. JEB Stuart) and played in the same woods and streams that James did. He served on the Board of Directors of the JEB Stuart Trust and was President for four years. He was instrumental in getting Laurel Hill, Stuart's birthplace, placed on the National Register of Historical Places and listed as one of Virginia's Historical Landmarks.

Dean is a watercolor artist and has used some of his interpretations as illustrations in *Boyhood Adventures of Gen. JEB Stuart, A Civil War Hero*. He is also known as a writer of humorous poems and historical articles in magazines and newspapers. Another book which he has written is *Rupert the Cross Eyed Rooster*, which tells the adventures of a rooster with the disability of having cross eyes. Dean says that all his stories teach a moral and are suitable for children as well as adults. *The Confederate Mouse* is a children's book, which tells how the simple field mice of northern Virginia helped the Southern Soldiers win the First

Battle of Manassas. *Grandma's Stories Cures, & Fixings From The Blue Ridge* are actual stories that Grandma Horton told to us children as we were growing up. Many family photographs, art work, and photographs of the Blue Ridge area by Mark Brown, Kate Brown and Mrs. Gail Josey, a long time family friend.

Dean is a retired teacher of 41 years; most of his time spent as a Librarian in maximum security prisons for youthful offenders and alternative schools for at-risk students in Florida, Virginia, and North Carolina. Dean attended Mount Airy Schools and graduated in 1957. He is a graduate of Appalachian State University of North Carolina. He did his graduate work in Criminal Psychology at the University of South Florida and also completed his graduate work in Library Science at Appalachian.

Dean Brown, Age 5
Author of Our Family History